Mirror, Mask, and Shadow

MIRROR, MASK,

The Risk and Rewards

SHELDON KOPP

AND SHADOW

of Self-Acceptance

MACMILLAN PUBLISHING CO., INC.
New York
COLLIER MACMILLAN PUBLISHERS
London

Macmillan Publishing Co., Inc.
866 Third Avenue, New York, N.Y.   10022
Collier Macmillan Canada, Ltd.

10   9   8   7   6   5   4   3   2   1

Library of Congress Cataloging in Publication Data

Kopp, Sheldon B   1929-
   Mirror, mask, and shadow.

   Includes bibliographical references.
   1. Self-acceptance.   I. Title.
BF697.K656   1981   158'.1   80-18626
ISBN 0-02-566460-3

Printed in the United States of America

We can satisfy in life a few of our passions and each passion but a little, and our characters indeed but differ because no two men bargain alike. The bargain, the compromise, is always threatened, and when it is broken we become mad or hysterical or are in some way deluded. . . .

—William Butler Yeats, *Mythologies*

Contents

Contents

Acknowledgments

Excerpts on pages v, 1, 51, 111, and 161 are taken from the following:

William Butler Yeats, *Mythologies* (p. 341). Published by Collier Books, New York, 1979.

George Seferis, "Argonauts," in *Mythical Story in Four Greek Poets: C. P. Cavafy, George Seferis, Odysseus Elytic, Nikos Gatsos* (p. 45). Poems chosen and translated from the Greek by Edmund Keeley and Phillip Sherrard. Published by Penguin Books, Harmondsworth, Middlesex, England, 1966. Used by permission.

James Thomson, "The City of Dreadful Night," in *Victorian and Late English Poets* (p. 1094), edited by James Stephens, Edwin L. Beck, and Royall H. Snow. Published by American Book Co., New York, 1934.

Walt Whitman, "Song of Myself," in *An Anthology of Famous English and American Poetry* (p. 666), edited and with introductions by William Rose Benét and Conrad Aiken. Published by Modern Library, Random House, Inc., New York, 1944.

Terence (12th century B. C.), *Heautontimoroumenos*, Act I.

Selection on pp. 125-127 from *The Dialogues of Plato*, translated by Benjamin Jowett (4th ed., 1953), Vol. I, pp. 521-24. Reprinted by permission of Oxford University Press.

Selection on p. 197 from "The Second Coming" from *COLLECTED POEMS of William Butler Yeats*, edited by M. L. Rosenthal, 1962, p. 91. Used by permission of A. P. Watt Ltd., London; and Macmillan Publishing Co., Inc., New York.

PART I

Mirror, Mask, and Shadow

And the soul,
If she is to know herself,
Must look
Into the soul:
The stranger and the enemy, we saw him in the mirror.

—George Seferis, "Argonauts"

CHAPTER 1

Where Did You
Get That Self?

*Having crossed the border into a foreign land, a young man
finds himself unexpectedly challenged by a local policeman.
The officer orders this stranger to identify himself. Readily
intimidated, the suspect politely states his name and his national-
ity, explaining defensively that he is simply a tourist, nothing
more.*

*The officer demands verification of this alleged identity. If
he is really who he says he is, the accused must produce his passport. Confidently, the defendant reaches into his breast pocket
but is shaken to find that it is empty.*

*Unable to produce proof of his innocence, he searches himself
more and more frantically. He begins to feel overwhelmed by
the panicky vision of ending up a condemned criminal. Then
all at once his alarm gives way to relief as he recalls placing his
passport on the bed-table while changing clothes to go out on
this ill-fated walk.*

*The stranger explains that he can produce proof of his iden-
tity if only the policeman will accompany him back across the*

[3]

border to his home. The officer does not believe his story. He accuses the suspect of pretending to be someone other than who he really is. If the defendant is to avoid being imprisoned for carrying on this masquerade, he must offer immediate and absolute proof that he is himself, and no one else.

Confused and frightened, the accused goes through his pockets once again. Perhaps during the first hasty search, the passport was somehow overlooked. He must have it with him somewhere. Otherwise how will the policeman know that it's really him, and not somebody else?

But in his pockets he can find only a partially soiled handkerchief, a small sum of local currency, and a candid snapshot of himself taken at the airport when he was leaving home to make this misbegotten holiday trip. In desperation, he thrusts the photograph into the officer's outstretched hand, pleading: "Just look right here at this picture. Surely you can see that it's me."

The policeman examines the snapshot with care, and then holds it up so he can compare it with the stranger's actual face. One look is all that is needed to satisfy him. Seeing that indeed it is a photograph of the tourist's own face, the officer is convinced that he must be exactly who he says he is.

The matter is settled. The young man is free to come and go as he pleases. The police officer apologizes for having raised any question about the other's identity: "Clearly you have nothing to hide. And, after all, how could you be mistaken about who you are?"

Most of the time the question doesn't even come up. Surely you know who you are as you know your own name. Imagine realizing that you might be mistaken about who you believe yourself to be. Each night you go to sleep fully confident that in the morning you will awaken to find that you are the same completely familiar person you were when you went to bed. So long as attention is not focused on your identity, you simply take for granted that there is no question about who you are. Being that same person is one of the few things in life that you can count on without worrying about it. *Or is it?*

Think back to those painful times when, like the young tourist, you have been caught off guard by someone else's discrediting challenge. Let yourself recall moments of embarrassment when your own unintended behavior revealed discrepancies between who you usually think of yourself as being and that seemingly less acceptable person you sometimes turn out to be.

Even when you are satisfied with the visible image of yourself, other people are not always willing to take you at face value. Inevitably, from time to time, the unexpected exposure of hidden flaws will be unavoidable. Any kind of disruption can result in that painfully uneasy refocusing of attention that we call *self-consciousness*. How vulnerable any of us can be made to feel when confronted by the deceptively simple question, Who am I?

Even though we all understand that each of us keeps secret from others a large portion of who we are, much of the time we try to act as though we have nothing to hide. Of course, no one is expected to go out in public exposing the true face of his or her early morning mirror reflection. That unadorned self is reserved for the private occasions of intimate meetings with trusted family members, personal friends, and selected lovers.

The mask worn by the social self is an attempt to live up to the collective standards, to be the sort of person the community expects us to be. Though these social disguises can be politically expedient, like any impersonation they consume needed creative energies. The more vigilance demanded by our surroundings, the less attention we can afford to give to exploration of our inner landscapes.

A formal ceremonial mask may be demanded when we face the social world. But even trusted personal relationships are rarely entered into with a completely open show of our true reflection unimproved by an attempt to hide the blemishes and otherwise enhance our attractiveness. Wearing this more revealing personal mask, we hide only those excesses and deficiencies that constitute the discrepancies between what we believe will be appealing to our loved ones and what we find unacceptable in ourselves. Each of us is aware of things about ourselves that

5

seem too awful to acknowledge to anyone else. Some thoughts and feelings are never openly expressed. Such secrets are willingly examined only in the safety of solitude.

You may be able to fool even those people who mean most to you. Knowing only those parts of you that you choose to reveal to them, they *seem* to care. But what would happen if they should discover what you are like when nothing is hidden in the shadows? If they *really* knew you, would they still care?

Letting your self be known means taking a chance, but hiding out can be just as risky. To the extent that you succeed in deceiving others, you are left stuck and alone with secret feelings that some others might be able to accept, and with hidden qualities that some might even value. And if no one knows you, then who can love you?

There are some losses even more damaging than missing out on other people's acceptance of who you are. The missed opportunities risked in deceiving others are slight compared with the needless suffering that comes from fooling yourself.

It may be tempting to try to dismiss all these questions about your self. After all, like the young tourist, surely you know who you are. It would seem that all of your life you've had a self and that you've always known exactly who you were.

As a matter of fact, the initial defining of who you were to be began *before* you were born. From the moment of conception you were already graced with all of your biologically predetermined constitutional characteristics (ranging from eye color to basic temperament). To these inborn parameters were added your waiting family's fantasy projections. Like all newborns, you soon satisfied their best wishes and worst fears about who they knew you would be. Very soon after your birth the myths that were to shape your life were announced and confirmed. ("See, he has grandpa's smile"; "she's such a good-natured baby"; "he's only happy when I'm holding him"; "she's never satisfied.")

Burdened or supported by your family's projections of disowned aspects of each of their own selves, whatever you did was

6

taken to be further confirmation of your already assigned identity. No matter how accepting any family might be, some perceptions of the new baby are sure to be unconsciously selective. How the infant is treated will also be overdetermined. Mothering[1] inevitably includes some inappropriate expressions of the parent's needs that are out of touch with what might best suit the baby at any particular time.

As a very young child you were exquisitely vulnerable to the shaping effects of your parents' behavior, including their projection of who it was all right for you to be. Though your waiting family experienced your *biological* birth as the sudden emergence of a new person, your own *psychological* birth[2] had not yet taken place. The beginnings of your consciousness and your growing sense of self began later and developed more gradually over an extended period of time.

Before you can know *who* you are, you first must learn *that* you are. During the earliest weeks after you were born, there was no particular need for you to distinguish where you ended and where the world outside began. These boundaries only gradually became important as you experienced the repeated frustrations of hunger and pain. Even these tensions would not have been enough to have forced the growing awareness of the distinction between you and not-you. This evolving consciousness depended on the gradual maturation of your capacities for clear perception and focused attention.

The earliest beginnings of differentiating yourself from the rest of the world were very primitive. After all, during the first few weeks of your life you were more often asleep than awake. Even when aroused, as a newborn infant you were largely unresponsive to stimuli from the outside world. Most of your day was spent in a half-sleeping, half-waking state occasionally uncomfortably alerted by hunger or other bodily discomforts. Once satisfied, you were easily ready to sleep again. Back then you were more a physiological creature than a psychological one. Even as this lack of recognition of anything outside of yourself eventually gave way to a dim awareness that your need

7

satisfactions were sometimes provided from somewhere outside, at first you were only able to maintain a fleeting responsiveness to these external stimuli.

During these first few weeks you had little more than bodily needs to satisfy. Had you known the terms *bad* and *good*, the first would have applied to hunger, cold, wet, pain, etc., and the second to their absence. Only gradually would your comforting become more and more associated with the ministrations of whoever mothered you.

By the second month of your life, this dim awareness expanded into the experience of a *symbiotic* phase that merged you and mother, almost as if you were not separate beings. But this blissful state of perfect union could not last. You needed her absolutely. Like every other mother, her need for the baby you were was relative and more limited. You were just beginning your infantile differentiation between what was "me" and what was "not-me," between what was contained within you and what and who was part of the outside world. No matter how tenderly mother loved you, as a grown-up she had long since ascertained where she ended and others began.

Gradually your omnipotent sense of fusion with mother had to give way. Again and again it was challenged by the many times when you cried hungrily and mother did *not* immediately appear to satisfy your need. In this way life painfully instructs each of us that we have a self and that its power is limited.

Except for these frustrating occasions, when you were awake happiness was seeing your mother's face. Especially when she was feeding you or talking to you, eye contact between you and mother was assurance that all was right with the world. This lovely state evoked your own first social smile.

You were four or five months old before you showed this crucial sign that a specific bond had been established between you and mother. You were now entering the beginning of the *differentiation* phase of the process of separation and individuation that would eventually allow you to develop that self whom you have since become.

8

Between that time and about the beginning of the third year of your life, you accumulated more and more memories of the "good" and "bad" experience of mother's comings and goings. Gradually you hatched psychologically into a more permanently alert sensory state whenever you were awake. This allowed you to start experimenting with the separation from mother necessary to developing a separate self of your own.

Exploring mother's face by looking and touching and putting food in her mouth, you began to pull back a bit from her so that you could begin to see her as "the other one." You played at separating by responding to her peekaboo games. To ease the pain of separation you held on to your baby blanket and other transitional objects that reminded you of mother.

Her preferred pattern of soothing or playing with you became your own ways of rocking and touching, so that you could feel as though mother was there with you even when you two were apart. Eventually this made it easier for you to leave her lap to crawl off to enter the world on your own.

When you were seven or eight months old you needed to be as close as possible to mother's feet and to check back with her from time to time. Sometimes you comfortably looked to her for reassurance. Other times you turned to her in panic. It was a time of comparing mother and other people, a time when, though still afraid of them, you became interested in strangers.

You were about to move out into the world as a separate individual. As you showed interest in doing this, if mother was sensitively encouraging, you gradually moved further and further away from her for longer and longer periods of time. From ten to twelve months old till you were about a year and a half, you entered the *practicing* phase of separation and self-development. Crawling, paddling, climbing, and standing, gradually you felt freer from mother and increasingly interested in the rest of the world. It was an exciting time, especially once you learned to walk upright and on your own. So began what some people call your "love affair with the world."

Despite moments of doubt and alarm, more and more of your

waking life became an adventure of exploring the world, mastering physical skills, and learning the pleasure of showing off. Now it was you who *actively* played peekaboo with mother, running off until she would sweep you up. Learning to wave bye-bye became more important than smiling hello.

Collective wisdom has it that a baby's first unaided steps are *toward* its mother. In reality you first began to walk while mother was out of the room or in a direction *away* from her. If mother felt comfortable about the separation, and confident that you would be able to make it out there in the world, she supported your exchanging the magic closeness with her for the pleasure of being on your own.

Except for those moments when your low-keyed longing was evoked by awareness that mother was gone, your growing self-esteem kept you happy with your freedom. It was during this time of growing independence that you went from being an infant to becoming a toddler. From the middle of the second year of your life, you were walking, talking, and eventually able to play out your fantasies symbolically.

More and more free, able, and on your own, you became increasingly aware of your separateness from mother. It was time to enter the third phase of the separation process, a time of *rapprochement*. While practicing your separate involvement with the world, temporarily you had set aside your need for continuing closeness with mother.

Toward the end of your practicing period it had begun to dawn on you that you were not really master of all you surveyed. More independent encounters with the physical world and with other people was often too much for you. Coping with it all on your own was sometimes overwhelming for a relatively helpless, so very small, and too separate person. This burden made it necessary to make a temporary nostalgic return to mother's powerful protectiveness. It was time to renegotiate that relationship in a way that would allow your continuing independence within the reassuring context of occasional reunion with the merging mother you once knew.

10

If you could work things out just right with her, you could be independent most of the time, while still able to get the help and relief you sometimes required. All of this depended on how flexible a transitional relationship you and mother could manage.

She would have had to be comfortable with your disruptive coming and going that reflected her toddler's continuously shifting needs. It was a difficult period of transition. At those times when you were safe and needed to manage on your own, mother had to be physically and emotionally available without being intrusive.

Nor was it an easy time for you. Your own mixed feelings about where you stood with mother were alternately expressed sometimes by shadowing her every move and then by darting away anytime she reached for you. She was always the favorite audience for your showing off. Again and again you would return from your busy activities in the world to bring her things, to show her what you could do, to ask her questions, and to give her answers.

You felt more indecisive and uncertain about yourself than you had for a long while. Once again you were afraid of strangers. Ironically, at the same time, you began to become more involved with the familiar figures in your world. Mother was no longer the only significant person in your life. Father became important enough so that sometimes you wanted to be like him. Other toddlers now meant more to you. Instead of just imitating them, you seemed to be able to care how they felt. As mother had taken care of you, you began to take care of yourself and others.

It was during this newly social phase of your development that you appeared to begin to judge the behavior of other people. This was especially evident in your reactions to separations, particularly expressed in your renewed difficulties with mother's leave-taking. If she was gone for a while, it was as if she became the "bad mother."

During those separations, you became preoccupied with longings for the fantasied "good mother." Paradoxically, when

11

mommy came back, usually you were too angry and disappointed to be glad to see her. She was not able to do anything right to ease your crankiness. All you could do was to demand of her, "What did you bring me?"

While she was away, you comforted yourself by underscoring your sense of power and control. You talked incessantly about *my* mommy and you took over her things as though they were your own. It was as though the more that was "mine," the more easily you were able to leave mother actively and on your own.

You had been out in the world on your own long enough to have gotten somewhat beyond your fear of losing mother altogether. Instead, during this time when you experienced her as either bad or good, you became fearful of losing her love. The most upsetting emotional crises during this time of your young life pivoted around your increased sensitivity to mother's approval and disapproval.

Your preoccupation with right and wrong was not restricted to how you and mother might judge each other. Your range of emotions was widening. Along with the beginnings of empathy for other toddlers, you expressed approval and disapproval of the appropriateness of their behavior. You also began to monitor your own expressions of sadness and anger. It was not until now that you could sometimes be seen checking your rage and trying to fight off your tears.

Your emerging awareness that you had a self required gradual differentiation from your original experience of merger with mother. Her sensitive *mirroring* of your emotional and physical needs (including your evolving movement toward becoming a separate person) allowed you to develop the inner psychological structures that supported that newfound sense of self.

Now you were learning when and how and to whom it was appropriate to reveal that self. Some expressions of feeling had to be hidden and others to be simulated if you were to gain approval and to avoid disapproval. It was a time of discovering which aspects of who you are were socially acceptable and which were not. If you were to gain the praise that made you feel so proud, and to avoid the shame of ridicule you dreaded, you would have to learn to disguise some of your feelings some of the time. You had to be able to be the person that *they* expected you to be. You had to learn the doctrine of the *mask*.

It is within this social process that you first developed your compliant false self. Defined by other people's expectations, the behavior of this social self was presented to meet what you imagined they wanted to see. For a time your self-confidence and your self-esteem depended largely on your experience of success or failure in meeting these external standards. You responded to your self as you saw others responding to you. It was necessary to hide your own identity behind a pose that would protect it from the punishment and humiliation that sometimes accompanied other people's disapproval. You knew that you had a self, but you were not yet sure just what that self was all about. Before that more personal core could clearly evolve, for a while it was necessary to let others tell you who it was all right for you to be.

The establishing of your own identity had first required that you differentiate enough from mother to become aware that you were a separate person. Next came the time of learning who you must appear to be in the eyes of others. Still to come was that open-ended phase that is to continue for the rest of your life: the development of that subjective sense of self that makes up the personal experience of what it's like to be you.

All of these developments were gradual and erratic. From the beginning differentiation out of the primary merger with mother to the eventual consolidation of your individuality, phases have overlapped in the irregular process of the natural growth of your consciousness of who you are.

The last, lifelong phase of self-definition had already begun by the time you were three years old. Out of this primitive transition from "me" into "I" you have developed a complex sense of just who you are, evolved a personal style of relating to other people, and participated in an exciting interplay of personality and values. It was at the beginning of this ultimate phase that you first sensed that in certain ways you are different from any-one else. To the extent that your parents were sufficiently appreciative of your personal needs in developing a self of your own, your individuality depended only minimally either on compliance with or rebellion against how your mother and father defined you and themselves.

It was during that third year of your life that the boundaries of your self became clear enough to give you a more stable sense of who you were. Your identity no longer depended so completely on what was going on between you and mother at any given moment. If the care you were given was adequately reliable, tender, and respectful, you came to be able to live with the ambiguity of both mother and you each being sometimes good and sometimes bad.

The comfort afforded by this perspective helped you to temper your hatred toward her and/or toward yourself at those inevitable times when the conflict between you two became intense. You learned to endure frustration without having to condemn or reject either one of you. Being on your own (without having to worry about who you were) became so enjoyable that you no longer had to experience mother as being bad just because she was sometimes absent.

Crises became less overwhelming as you developed this perspective on mother and you having separate, imperfect, and yet acceptably good enough selves. However, before it could be firmly established, the gradual development of this comforting overview was punctuated by many setbacks. For a long while, both your individual sense of self and the constancy of your acceptance of this imperfect mother remained fluid and reversible achievements.

Many other factors contributed to your growing capacity for tolerating delayed gratification and for enduring separation. As you became better able to translate your wishes, ideas, and feelings into words, you became more and more effective at communicating your needs and getting them fulfilled. As your fantasy life developed, by playing make-believe you become

14

increasingly able to compensate for the world's imperfections (and for your own). Your growing interest in relating to playmates and to other grown-ups slowly diminished mother's crucially central significance in your life.

All of these maturing functions contributed to the growing psychological space you needed for the achievement of your individuality. When you found yourself with too little space, you could begin to fight for it actively by resisting the oppressive demands of grown-ups. You could be as stubbornly negativistic as was required to preserve a separate sense of who you were. Increased mastery of communication, understanding, fantasy, and reality testing all contributed to your keeping in mind a self other than what other people expected you to be.

Gradually establishing your individuality meant that again you had to learn to distinguish between one aspect of experience and another. During the first few months of your life, you began to find out that you existed apart from your mother. At first you had experienced the two of you as one. Slowly you differentiated the boundaries where you ended and the outside world began.

Now, developing a stable sense of what it meant to be you required separating out your subjective inner self from the social behaviors that you began to display to meet other people's expectations. But there was a third sort of differentiation yet to be made.

First you had learned to distinguish the "me" from the "not-me." Next you had to learn to be clear about the difference between your compliant social self and your untamed private self. At last you were ready to begin distinguishing between the "I" and the "not-I." It was then that you began developing the *ego* that would someday represent the center of your conscious adult personality.

Some other aspects of your total self would remain acceptable while others would have to be disavowed. This distinction was determined largely by your childhood interactions with parents and a few other significant people. In a general way your family acted as societal agent for reinforcing the values of the subculture

15

of which you were all a part. But more crucial to whom you would turn out to be were your parents' less conscious, more personal behavior patterns, their own internal conflicts and unconscious fantasies. Beyond your awareness (or theirs), these more hidden personality factors would crucially affect which parts of your self you would someday comfortably accept and which parts unwittingly you would disown.

The differences in our constitutional predispositions may make some modes of experiencing and behaving more probable in one person than in another.[3] Even so, surely we are all potentially capable of a full range of human wishes, feelings, thoughts, and actions.

Whatever your own inborn predispositions, certain early experiences determined what sort of options resulted in your feeling safe, satisfied, and happy, and which threatened you with destruction, deprivation, and despair. Those aspects of your original self that brought about the more nurturing situations became consciously identified as your own. But not all of your responses were acceptable to your parents. Some they consciously viewed as not good for you. Others unconsciously evoked reflections of your parents' own selves that they could not bear to know.

To those of your responses that upset your parents beyond their emotional tolerance, they reacted in ways that eliminated (or at least minimized) that behavior. If even their imagining your going on with whatever disturbed them elicited enough of their anxiety, you were treated in ways that made those parts of your self too dangerous for you to even think about. Soon these thoughts (plus much of whatever else might arouse them) were disowned as "not-I" and relegated to the shadowy realm of your unconscious.

This is how you came to be the conscious self you are. The process required disavowal of unacceptable impulses and of their representations in fantasy. So too this is how you came to have a hidden self that does not seem like you at all.

We each must find ways of dealing with the conflicts and con-

16

tradictions inherent in our dual, or perhaps even multiple natures. Every acknowledged attitude has as its counterpart an equally substantial polar opposite. The more extreme the attitude, the more exaggerated, undifferentiated, and out of touch its hidden equivalent. Unless we become acceptingly aware of those unconscious *shadow* sides of who we are, we are certain to find ourselves at the mercy of their powerfully primitive demands.

Remaining unconscious of these disowned parts of ourselves is both costly and dangerous. No matter how much we limit our experience in the service of protecting their inner constraints, we can never fully eliminate the risk of episodic outbreak of the forbidden impulses. In any case, demands that are not faced within ourselves will be confronted unexpectedly in the world about us.

The inner forces for which we do not take responsibility narrowly limit our options and destructively control our lives. When faced as projections onto the outside world, these disowned selves are always experienced as larger than life-size. We may find such a second self disgusting, terrifying, or enthralling. Surely we will find it unmanageable.

This book emerged out of my search for fuller awareness of my own hidden selves. In it, I draw on a lifelong game of hide-and-seek with the dark side of myself, on desperate attempts to avoid facing all of who I am, and on learning to risk being more conscious and self-accepting, sometimes.

In the darkness of their own projected shadows, many of the people who come to me for psychotherapy have lost sight of joy and meaning. If they are to attain some measure of power over their own lives and to renew their options for happiness, they have to risk discovering that neither I nor they are just what we say we are, and even less are we what we have been taught we should be. My accounts and explorations of the risks and rewards of self-acceptance come from my work with these patients[4] and from my personal life, out of their struggles and my own.

NOTES, CHAPTER 1

1. For simplicity's sake, I will use the terms *mother* and *mothering* throughout to indicate the provision of continuing primary personal care of infants and toddlers. Obviously this need not imply the actual, biological mother. This care may be provided by someone who is neither female nor even a natural parent.

2. Margaret S. Mahler, Fred Pine, and Annie Bergman, *The Psychological Birth of the Human Infant: Symbiosis and Individuation* (New York: Basic Books, Inc., 1975). I have borrowed freely from the developmental categories described by Dr. Mahler and her associates.

3. This includes the primitive preferences for one sensory modality over another, for verbal vs. nonverbal responses, for active or passive modes of adaptation, and perhaps for rudimentary temperamental inclinations.

4. All accounts of patients are disguised to protect their privacy. In some instances the portraits I have presented are composites. In others, identifying biographical details have been omitted or changed.

CHAPTER 2

My Own Dark Brother

Many of the unhappy people who come to me for psychotherapy suffer just as I have from painful problems of severely limited self-acceptance. My job is to help them get to know themselves more fully. In an accepting, nonjudgmental atmosphere, gradually patients may come to feel safe enough to face the hidden aspects of who they are. With this increased self-understanding comes greater self-acceptance.

As this occurs, the range of personal freedom expands, minimizing the needless suffering that is the price of defensive denial of parts of themselves. Greater acceptance of who they are allows them opportunities for a richer, sweeter life.

No one is totally self-accepting. Irreconcilably opposing forces within our contradictory conscious/animal natures, further complicated by the antagonistic needs of the group and the individual, burden every human being with a personality that is at least partially divided against itself. Damaging childhood experiences leave some people more severely divided than the rest.

In the interest of better understanding the nature of their divided selves and the relative severity of their suffering, we can roughly classify these people into three categories of personality damage: *psychotic*, *borderland* and *neurotic*.[1] Abusive parenting during the first months of life can shatter irreparably the capacity for developing a cohesive sense of self. The terror of threatened annihilation results in a shattered self that may be *psychotic* from infancy on, or later lapse into chronically incapacitating madness.

Some children start out with good enough parenting. As infants and young toddlers, they do not yet pose a threat to their neurotic parents. This gives these children the freedom and support needed to develop a cohesive sense of who they are. Later on some of these seemingly accepting parents react to the child's sexuality and aggression as if these instinctual displays were dangerously explosive forces in need of tight control. The threatened parents set up unduly harsh injunctions. Fear of punishment (internalized as guilt) results in disavowal of the problematic instincts. Defenses are developed to bolster the wall of repression with which the *neurotic* maintains the horizontal division between the idealized conscious self and its unacceptable primitive impulses.

Some divided personalities were neither subjected to abuse so early and severe as to shatter their capacity for an adaptive self nor allowed to develop a self only to be cruelly taught later that they were not to have any fun. Instead, during the first two to three years, these children were merely treated impersonally. Situational or parental needs took priority in a way that obscured what the particular child might need. In response to repeated intrusion and neglect, the child had to learn to set aside its own needs. The only way to establish a manageable environment was to contrive a false self that would take care of the needs of the self-absorbed mothering one. As grown-ups, these *borderland* personalities maintain a vertical division between the contrived hollowly compliant false self and the archaic shamelessly grandiose true self. Maintaining this division makes for a vulnerable posture, an uncertain identity, and an empty life.

From the outset I know that some of my patients' difficulties date from earliest stirrings and shaping of what they now know as their troubled selves. They cannot remember those experiences of the first months of their lives any more than you or I can recall our own beginings. Even once their attention had first become better defined, conceptual capacities for symbolic imagery and for language were not yet developed as a means of recording experiences.

If my patients are to attain the rewards of self-acceptance, I must try to help them to understand how they came to be who they are. But as it is not possible to remember those earliest experiences that so crucially affected the shaping of the self, together we must reconstruct the past, based in part on inferences drawn from the kind of self the patient has had to invent.

In the task of inventing a self, everything works for a little while. Nothing works for very long. My parents set my task by defining me as a "bad boy" who could become anything he really wanted to be. But my adolescent efforts to become a desperado never quite worked. I guess my heart wasn't really in it. More an outcast than an outlaw, I soon became a deficient delinquent. Episodically I mingled at the margins of any adventure that I imagined could qualify as being exotic, savage, or—at the very least—indulgent. Between what I hoped were "debaucheries," I hurried back to Mommy and Daddy's house to do my homework.

For a time I was certain I had fooled almost everyone. But instead of making me feel good, this success left me disturbingly uneasy. What if someday they all really got to know me? Would anyone accept me then? Worse yet, self-deception had turned my life into a frenzied alternation between sacrificially working at working and superficially playing at playing.

It was just as my parents had always told me: I could never get anything right. Not only was I a disappointment to them, but to myself. By the time I reached twenty, the secretly studious "good boy" aspect of my divided self had become dominant. I was now a compulsively driven, overachieving graduate student. Knowing that I was only fooling my professors into believing that I was worthwhile in their terms, I continued to strive to impress my peers that I was really a rebelliously unmanageable, self-directed young anarchist. My hypocrisy ran in both directions. Whenever I turned up in a Greenwich Village coffee shop, you could be sure that I had already secretly completed my studies and assignments for that week.

It was during this phase of my masquerade that I entered psychotherapy as a patient for the first time. Integrity and commitment were my guiding principles, tension and depression my psychiatric symptoms. At the time, falling asleep each night was impossible until I had first reviewed everything that I had accomplished that day, and unlikely unless the list seemed sufficiently impressive to warrant deserved rest.

Each morning, I awoke to the same first conscious thought, "Today is Monday." Even before checking it out I would be dimly aware that six to one it was *not* Monday. My knowing that this obsessional thought was irrational did not make it go away. My understanding of this morbid mantra was limited to the benevolent interpretation that it simply meant that I viewed each day as an opportunity to begin anew. By then I had begun to mellow my tarnished self-image with an idealized patina.

I could do this by invoking the idealized romantic image of myself that I kept in reserve for such occasions. Without much conviction, I would reassure myself that I was ever ready to take on whatever challenges life might provide. It was hard to face the fact that taking on difficult tasks was less a matter of heroism than a way of distracting myself from life's many temptations to waste my time just having fun.

During the course of my first session with the therapist, I reviewed my problems systematically, anticipated his questions about my family background, and gave what I intended to be a brilliant autobiographical case history. At the conclusion of my presentation, I was upset by the realization that I had left something out.

Apologetically I added: "Doctor, there is one additional complication in my clinical picture. I should have brought it up earlier but I guess I repressed it. The point is . . . what I didn't tell you is that . . . sometimes I believe that I am developing schizophrenia."

Without fully masking his amusement, the therapist allowed that for a clinical psychology graduate student like myself incipient schizophrenia must be an interesting problem to have. He suggested that I confirm my diagnosis by describing all of my clearly prepsychotic symptoms. At that moment, what I wanted more than anything else in the world was to be able to offer incontrovertible proof that my catastrophic prognosis was correct. I was painfully embarrassed to discover that I could not cite a single clearly indicative symptom to support my differential diagnosis.

At that point the therapist intervened, saving me from what felt like the humiliation of being called on in class when I had not done my homework. He interrupted my apologies saying, "That's all right. Never mind the incipient symptoms you've had so far. They're often unclear this early in such syndromes. Instead why don't you tell me what you imagine it will be like when you become a full-blown schizophrenic."

Up to that moment my apprehensions had been restricted to the *idea* of becoming psychotic. His suggestion suddenly allowed my consciousness to be flooded with fantasied experience of just what it would be like to have my imagined breakdown.

I tried to communicate how alien it all now seemed to me, saying, "It would be just awful. They would certify that I was not responsible for my actions and lock me away for the rest of my life. I'd be put out of graduate school and lose my job. They'd keep me in a place where I couldn't work. I'd be so helpless, the staff would have to feed me and bathe me and put me to bed. All I would be able to do for myself is to sit around sucking my thumb. I couldn't stand living like that—could I?"

By the time I finished my description, the horrors of being reduced to infantile dependency had begun to seem curiously appealing. Just then the therapist interrupted my reveries with the unexpectedly disappointing reassurance, "I don't think that there is any need for you to worry that you will ever actually become a schizophrenic."

He went on to explain: "What you have is a moderately dis-

23

tressing, nondisabling garden variety neurosis. There's little chance of your ever becoming so severely disturbed that you would be forced to let someone else take care of you. In any case, having to go crazy before you are allowed to rest is no way to take a vacation.

"Together we could explore your feeling compelled to work so hard. Perhaps some day you can get to accept your neediness fully enough to allow yourself to take it easy without first having to lose your mind. After that you'll have the remainder of your life to work on getting better and better at being able to play without having to worry about accomplishing great things."

Almost thirty years later, at times I find that I still have to struggle with that one. At first I imagined it would be a matter of waking up one morning to the thought "Today is Sunday," knowing that my work was finished, seeing that it was good, and that now I could rest.

It took a while for me to realize that it would mean waking up without immediately having to decide what day it was, and understanding that it is up to me to choose work or play as I please. If I should choose to play when practical considerations might make it wiser for me to work, I *might* have to face unpleasant situational consequences. But any time I work when I really need to play, I am sure to pay a damagingly high personal price.

It was a good deal later in our relationship before I could confess to the therapist just what an irresponsible wastrel I believed I really was underneath all that hypocritical display of good intentions and hard work. I told him of my secret fascination with evil and of how I felt drawn to wildly decadent characters. Editing here and there, I even went so far as to expose my perverted sexual fantasies.

Having developed that sinister portrait, at last I was able to challenge his benign diagnosis of me as an ordinary neurotic. Triumphantly, I summoned him to a second contest, declaring, "Maybe I won't ever become a schizophrenic. But just because I'll never get crazy enough for someone else to have to take care of me doesn't mean I'll have to go on working so hard to prove I'm good enough to deserve my parents' loving me. By now you must see that what I really have to worry about is becoming a psychopath!"

Again he was able to communicate his amused acceptance without exposing me to ridicule. Softly and sympathetically he responded by telling me, "You may spend the rest of your life easing out from under that burden of superintegrity you've had to take on. Perhaps you'll be able to cut it down to no bigger than life-size. Just don't expect to become irresponsible enough to go around destructively doing whatever you please, acting out all your secret impulses without any consideration for principle or for the rights of other people."

For a long while I resisted his reassurance that I was unlikely to come to a bad end. Later I realized that he was right. Even now, a lifetime later, I still struggle to reclaim the dark parts of myself that childhood survival demanded that I disavow. It was only five years ago when I first understood that I must someday write this book. It was then that I had my clearest dream encounter with the shadow of my own hidden self.[2]

I dreamed that I was on Cape Ann, the northern headland of Boston Bay. My own cape, where I most often spend my summers, is the southern head, Cape Cod, and the lovely islands that surround it. The southern cape is warm and rich and green and soft, but not so Cape Ann. The north cape is very different. I've spent time on the north cape and there are qualities about it that draw me back, but for the most part it has been a place that I have avoided. Cape Ann is a rugged, craggy seascape; angular, covered with scant, scrubby foliage; dark, windblown, dangerous-looking territory—in its own way a strikingly beautiful seascape, but very ominous.

The dream began with my having emerged from a small rugged beach cottage such as one might find on Cape Ann. I stepped through the doorway of the cottage and out into the night. I don't know where I was headed, but I began to walk slowly across a great open barren wilderness, a vast tundra. I followed the ambling footpaths; there were no roads. I wandered for a while and had come quite a distance from the cottage.

Suddenly the night became very, very dark. I don't know now whether I realized this in the dream or whether it came as an explanation I offered myself after I had awakened, but it seemed to me that the moon had suddenly fallen behind dark clouds. As I stood there in the sullen darkness, unable to see which way to go, a piece of my everyday anxiety suddenly flooded the dream. One of the difficulties in my recent life, a residual from brain surgery undergone several years ago, is that my balance is very uncertain. Taken by the inertia of my own movement, I am inclined to topple over. My body compensates for this during the day and although I suffer from some fatigue as a consequence, I can make my way. But at night when it's dark, my kinesthetic feedback is limited, distorted, betraying. Without daytime's visual cues, I need to carry a light or to hold someone's hand. Holding someone's hand was a difficult surrender for me. For a while I stubbornly resisted that. I no longer do so.

In the dream when I found myself in the darkness, suddenly I felt like a fool. I said to myself, "What the hell are you doing out here without a flashlight? How stupid to leave the house without the light that you needed." For a moment I stood there and debased myself for having made a mistake. Then I decided I must go back to the house, I must get a light, or I simply wouldn't be able to manage. I was afraid I would stumble, fall and hurt myself, or worse yet, that I would get lost forever on that vast dark plain. I tried to find my way back to the house. I couldn't see at all. I moved my feet, shuffling them about, trying to find the footpath. I found that just feeling about with my feet I couldn't really tell where the path was. Like an animal, I got down on all fours. Padding around with my hands I tried to discover where the path lay so that I could find my way back to the house.

While I was scrounging around down there, I became aware of another presence. I was not alone. At first I thought that it must be a dog. I need to say here that I respond counterphobically to my anxiety about dogs, anxiety that I don't understand and of which I am only inferentially aware. I don't know it directly. Dogs don't *seem* to frighten me, but I know that I am a bit rougher with them than I need to be. Rather than make friends, I try to intimidate them. At any rate, if this was a dog, it was only a dog, and I wasn't too upset about that.

Still, I remained on the alert. As I watched, the beast drew closer. Soon I could see the intense gleam of his glaring, yellow eyes. All at once I knew that it was not a dog. The beast I faced was a wolf.

Characteristically, I reacted as in my waking life. The first thing that occurred to me was, "Oh, I see, now my task is to kill this wolf." But then uncharacteristic things began to happen in the dream. I suddenly had a new look at myself and I thought, "That's absurd. It's too crazy! How can I kill a wolf with my bare hands, on his turf, in the darkness, at a time when I can't even walk with safety?"

And then came a second, still more startling wave of revelation. Suddenly I had a new understanding of what I must do. I knew then that *I must make friends with this wolf.*

At that point the dream ended and I awoke—awoke to feel that a door had opened to an unexplored part of my self. I do not know where this will lead. I both hope and dread meeting that wolf again, that wolf who is my own savage soul, the terror in my heart, my secret shadow. And yet, God help me, I *must* learn to give up what's left of my pose of being able to meet any challenge without feeling frightened. I must discard the false mask of mastery that goes with always having to seem able to overcome my terror. Instead I must learn to yield to it, to own it, to make friends with it, to come to love the rest of myself when next I encounter that *wolf* who is *my own dark brother.*

NOTES, CHAPTER 2

1. Psychodiagnostically, these categories each include a number of sub-patterns of suffering: (a) *psychotic*: infantile autism and childhood schizophrenia, adult and adolescent schizophrenic and manic-depressive psychoses (although among these patients there may be many whose problems are

organic or genetic in origin); (b) *borderland*: narcissistic, schizoid, paranoid, "borderline," psychopathic, and certain depressive character disorders; (c) *neurotic*: obsessive-compulsive, hysterical, phobic, and some depressive styles of living.

2. Sheldon B. Kopp, *The Hanged Man: Psychotherapy and the Forces of Darkness* (Palo Alto, Calif.: Science and Behavior Books, Inc., 1974), pp. 146–149. This dream was described here earlier, though in a somewhat different context.

CHAPTER 3

Beside Myself

Encounters with the shadowy figures in your dreams offer opportunities for reclaiming some disavowed aspects of your own
divided self. But the dream is only one of many avenues of
access. When you are under stress, your hidden self may appear
in any unguarded gateway. The intruder may appear whenever
inner and outer pressures combine to disarm or otherwise over-
whelm your conscious sentinels of reason and consistency. Like
an illegitimate child who finds its denying parent vulnerable,
your usually disowned self may seize the opportunity to claim its
rightful place in your life.

One time or another, everyone is unintentionally revealed
by a slip of the tongue. By now we are sophisticated enough
to interpret these momentary lapses of control as evidence of the
brief breakthrough of some bit of long-ago repressed unconscious
instinctual urge. Embarrassment yields quickly to parlor-psy-
choanalytic discounting of the personal exposure as no more
than a familiar instance of the universal fallibility of human
nature. "A Freudian slip," we smilingly reassure each other,
colluding to make no more of it.

Encountering evidence of the presence of the double who is

your own dark brother (or sister) is a more compelling experience, not so easily dismissed. The power of such a meeting does not evoke the simple embarrassment that goes with making a mistake. It moves you beyond the awkwardness of momentarily having lost possession of yourself, to the awesome sense that you may be irretrievably possessed.

Even minor manifestations of the second self challenge who you are. Remember all those times that you had thoughts or feelings so foreign to your conscious self-image that the contradiction demanded immediate reassurance? Wherever that stuff came from, certainly it was not from the *real* you! You found yourself saying, "What a crazy idea!" or "What an awful way for anyone to feel!" "That's not like me at all," you assured your conscious everyday reasonable and consistent self.

There have even been times when your double has taken over so completely that the disruption amounted to much more than mere internal possession by some unacceptable passing thought or feeling. At least briefly it was as if you became someone else. How could you have acted the way you did? Even now, it's still uncomfortable just remembering how you behaved.

The only way to live with some of what you've done is to insist that it was not really you. In order to establish that it was a case of mistaken identity, you explain, "I was not myself that day," or "I was beside myself."

Those times when your shadow side threatens to take over, you may express your distress by crying out that you feel as though you are "coming apart" or that you are "going to pieces." You may be driven to disown the encounter as a time when "I must have been out of my mind." Even pleading temporary insanity can seem less discrediting than acknowledging some unacceptable aspect of who you are.

It's not easy to admit that you are capable of thoughts, feelings, and behavior so foreign to the way you usually think of yourself. But, like it or not, the personal ego that establishes your everyday conscious image of who you are represents only a small portion of everything that makes up your self. The rest of you is hidden

30

in the shadows of your unconscious. Not that your shadow is made up of nothing but forbidden evil impulses. It simply includes all the personal characteristics that your conscious personality cannot acknowledge.

Some aspects of your shadow have been defined by the values of any group with which you identify as a member. In your family, subculture, or religious community, particular kinds of human behavior may be absolutely unacceptable. In that case, these hidden aspects of your self will be stored away in a collective shadow.[1] You will think, *"We* don't do that sort of thing. *They* do." The "they" upon whom the collective shadow is projected may refer to outsiders in general. Because they are not like us, we may shun them to avoid their bad influence. Worse yet, we may try to convert them so that they do not serve even as temptations.

In every society, some subgroups and individuals are singled out as "the others." We hound and scorn these poor bastards for doing those things that we cannot accept as part of ourselves. The marginal people upon whom we project the collective shadow of the accepted "us" include less powerful, underprivileged and oppressed subcultures. In this shadow also stand the deviants and outcasts whom we scorn, punish, and use as objects of our fantasies. We attempt to constrain them, to punish them, and to rehabilitate them. In other words, we try to make them over into a reflection of our acceptable picture of ourselves. Once incarcerated, these deviants will have to demonstrate even purer behavior than those of us who remain outside the walls of the prisons and the mental hospitals.

Not all that you disavow is hidden in this collective shadow. You have a personal shadow as well. In it are hidden all of those ideas, feelings, and wishes whose expression would have placed in jeopardy your most significant early childhood relationships. Helpless and dependent as you were as a small child, you could not have risked irrevocably offending the powerful people who took care of you. Nor could you have survived without developing a consistent and disciplined ego. You had no choice but to

31

disown those parts of yourself that threatened your life-supporting relationships. It was unsafe even to be aware of their existence.

The more threatening anything about you was to one of your parents, the more completely it would have had to be repressed. Focusing for the moment on oversimplified characteristics of human behavior from which you might have had to select, we can imagine your conscious personality being shaped to exclude one side or another of the polarities of being passive or aggressive, verbal or action oriented, intellectual or emotional, controlled or impulsive. Ironically, the more one-sided your conscious self became, the more one-sided your double's unconscious countertendencies would have to be.

Gradually your personal shadow became a repository of the negative side of your personality. That is not to say that it includes only characteristics that are bad or worthless. It simply means that in this shadow are hidden those parts of you that some significant early family member seemed to find unacceptable. In response, you learned to ignore that part of you that did not fit with the idealized image of yourself necessary to survival in that setting.

Those tendencies that are relegated to your shadow remain "somewhat inferior, primitive, unadapted, and awkward; not wholly bad."[2] You have learned to consider them evil, or at least sinister. They are, instead, merely the rest of you. Together, you and your shadow make a complete self. Though your shadow may contain some destructive potential, it also embodies lost vitality, highly personal creative possibilities, and everything you always wanted to know about yourself but were afraid to ask.

You may successfully keep some parts of yourself hidden in the dark, but you will not be able to avoid casting that shadow onto others about you. Projecting your shadow is *not* simply a matter of taking something that you deny in yourself and imagining it to be out there in a world in which it does not really exist. More often, what happens is this. You encounter in someone else something that you deny in yourself. The negative feelings that your conscious self holds toward your hidden self have been projected onto that other person. Whenever you find yourself feeling self-righteous, you are in the midst of such a projection.

It's not just a matter of making a moral judgment about someone else's behavior. Your reaction is out of proportion.

You discover that someone has sexual preferences radically different from what appeals to you. "My God, that's weird!" you think. "How could anyone be turned on by doing that?" you go on. "We should lock up people who act like that and throw away the key."

Harshness is not the only evidence of the disproportion of your reaction. You are deeply concerned about something that is not really any of your business. You find that even though the thought of such behavior makes you feel awful, somehow you simply cannot stop thinking about it. Again and again the distasteful act comes to mind. Again and again you reassure your conscious self that *you* could not possibly enjoy anything like that.

The more identified you are with your conscious personality, the less you will be aware of your shadow. When confronted with someone else's living out some aspect of being human that you experience as totally alien, you will be as self-righteous as is required to maintain the disavowal.

You may unconsciously select other people to act out aspects of your own hidden self, or even encourage others to behave in ways that serve you as an alter ego. If it meets the other person's needs, he or she may at the same time be using you as a reciprocal shadow. How many couples live Laurel and Hardy lives, each a caricature of the other's disowned self?

You may still value some of the positive qualities that early childhood experiences forced you to disown. This will result in your having a bright shadow[3] as well as a dark one. For example, self-assertiveness might have been defined as worthwhile, but just not your style. If so, you are likely to discover heroic figures in your life. Projecting onto them the positive regard for that

33

disclaimed part of yourself, you will idealize these people as always in the right when they stand up for themselves.

If you have been subjected to a thoroughgoing purging of unacceptable parts of yourself, you may have turned out to be one of those too-good-to-be-true people who believe that they cast no shadow. Though you can admit that "no one is perfect," you find it difficult to recall a time when you yourself were clearly in the wrong. If this is your posture, you are in a dangerous position. Whatever you have been unwilling or unable to face within yourself, you risk running into head-on in the world around you.

Though I have long been aware of this risk, much of the time simply knowing the dangers that lurked in the shadows without has not been enough to enable me to peer into the darkness within. Even during those periods when I felt safe enough and strong enough to pursue finding out more about myself, confusion and isolation often accompanied my efforts. Sometimes my loneliness felt more bearable because of the support and instruction I received from reading other people's tales of encounter with the specter of the hidden self. In this book, I have regathered some of these tales so that others may see what I saw. Together we may yet learn to risk more willingly the expanded personal consciousness that makes self-acceptance possible.

This risk can be avoided by clinging to the limited consciousness that accompanies unexamined everyday experience. It offers a vision of life divided into powerful polar forces, basically separate from one another and endlessly in opposition. By their very nature, the forces of light and darkness, of good and evil, and of life and death, seem fated to remain continuously in conflict. These struggles are experienced as going on within us as well as in the world in which we live. Some aspects of the inner struggles we own as self, or at least we claim them as familiar friends. Others we disclaim as not-self. These we project, encounter as strangers, or condemn as enemies.

When we acknowledge all the opposing forces as existing within us, they turn out to be as resistant to reconciliation as their counterparts in the world about us. It seems that there can be no lasting peace. Even when the good guys appear to be winning for a while, too soon, the tide of battle shifts. Once again, despair replaces hope as their unending alternation continues.

The need to reconcile the apparent contradictions in human nature finds voice in literature throughout recorded history and in all parts of the world.[4] From the earliest myths to contemporary television programming we witness our inescapable fascination with the conflicting dualities of life.

Though we have shifted to modern metaphors, today's tales of gods and demons still serve as projections of the warring powers within us. The enduring themes express implicit recognition that these psychic forces must be acknowledged or they will destroy us.

Some early literary attempts at forced reconciliation appeared as composite creatures of a dual nature. These mythic hybrids most often turned out to be monstrous menaces such as the minotaur, the mermaid, and the sphinx. Even among the oldest tales, such awkward metaphors soon yielded to representations of life's opposing forces as separate antagonists, wedded only in their eternal conflicts.

Among the less conscious of these literary projections are the epic tales of war between good and bad nations or between worthy and unworthy feuding families. The further removed from individual experience, the safer the tales. When the struggle has been externalized, the reader (or listener) can comfortably cheer for the forces of good and despise the forces of evil without understanding that both sides are contained within the self.

When the projections are less remote, the audience will find reading such tales a more disturbingly personal experience. It becomes easier to identify these conflicts as our own when they are characterized as struggles between twins (or at the very least, between siblings). It is difficult to take the relationships of Cain and Abel, or of Gilgamesh and Enkidu, as simple adventure stories having nothing to do with our own particular lives.

Projections of the divided self occur in many forms throughout

35

the history of story-telling. It is only within the last two hundred years that literature provides its most personal metaphor to date, the shadowy character of the Double.[5] An encounter with this disturbingly familiar figure defies dismissal as an experience unrelated to the reader's self.

The Double may take many forms. In one story he[6] is an imposter who tries to replace the major character. In another he appears as the protagonist's reflection, his shadow, or his portrait. The Double may even be a creation of the protagonist, or a creature into which he is transformed.

In some variations, the second self may appear clearly as an external reality, completely independent of and lacking any continuity with the first self. In that representation, the Double is more a second than a self. At the other extreme, the Double is clearly no more than a fantasy or a hallucination who shares a basic psychological identity with the protagonist but lacks any external reality of his own. Such a Double is a self, but not quite a second.

In those stories of the second self that readers find most disturbing, it is not possible to decide whether the Double is an actual physical duplicate or simply a creature of the imagination. It is just this unresolvable ambiguity that puts the reader in touch with personal experiences of having encountered his or her own shadow.

The bond between the first and the second self is always that same curious combination of antagonism and attraction that characterizes the ego's relationship with its shadow. Despite the first self's wish to dismiss the Double, they remain preoccupied with one another. Because it is easier to see out of the shadows than into them it cannot be a simple peer relationship. The second self often has mysteriously intimate understanding of the personality of first self, while the first self experiences the other as unfathomably strange. Their shared psychological territory may be as astonishing to the protagonist as it is to the reader.

Both in the literature of the Double and in the psychological experience of the shadow, the second self retains an uncanny aura. Despite its terror, like a bird watching a snake, the fascinated first self remains transfixed. Because the second self possesses secrets that the first self cannot ever quite fathom, the stranger remains the stronger of the two, always subtly in control of the relationship.

Like the personal shadow, the literary second self is that part of the hero that does not fit his conscious self-image. Just as the ego tries to deny or flee its shadow, the first self attempts to ignore or to escape from the Double. But like the shadow, the Double is that opposite that must be dealt with. If the first self does not find a way to come to terms with the second self, he risks remaining half a person.

The attitudes of the first self toward the second parallel the ego's reactions to the projections of its shadow. The other may be experienced with terror, revulsion, fascination, hatred, or love. Whatever the form of the positive or negative attitude toward the Double, it is sure to be filled with emotional tension. Whether the second self is experienced primarily as an object of longing or of dread, their meeting will evoke in the first self a sense of vulnerability, of inexplicable intimacy, of emotional intensity, and finally of inescapability.

In literature, as in life, the first self stands in the foreground of consciousness as the primary, familiar, central aspects of the person. The second self is experienced as auxiliary, alien, and at best as a complementary counterpart. The mutual preoccupation of one self with the other is an uneasy one. Dark, uncanny, and inexplicable, it remains ever tense, even potentially explosive.

From the point of view of the first self, all of this takes place as if in the unreal atmosphere of a semidream state. As readers, we never know just how this is experienced by the second self. The Double threatens us with its intuitive prior knowledge just as it does the protagonist.

Even so, the first self's involuntary affinity to the mysterious second self often invites the other to intrude. Like someone almost remembered, the Double can neither be fully owned nor disowned. He seems simultaneously familiar and unfamiliar. This uncanniness serves as both a barrier and a bond.

The second self cannot be dismissed as simply evil. Though

37

the first self may be afraid the Double will harm him, he also comes to understand that instead their meeting may turn out to be wonderfully helpful. Like our own everyday encounters with the projections of the disowned parts of ourselves, whenever the first self faces the Double there is an opportunity for the first self's growth. In disrupting the first self's comfortable complacency, the Double offers the opportunity for moving beyond self-deception to the personal freedom that comes with self-acceptance.

For this growth to occur, the first self must surrender his illusions of being reasonable and consistent so that the two may merge and become one. He must be willing to endure the agonized self-awareness that accompanies such psychological transformations. This will require his discovery that he must first accept being less than he believed he was if he is ever to become more than he has been.

Perhaps in their personal lives, people have always been faced with resolving critical problems of self-acceptance.[7] It is only recently that these struggles have become consciously explicit in our story-telling traditions. Before writers could introduce this new focus, certain changes in social and psychological perspectives had to occur. A complex interplay followed between artistic vision and intellectual insight, as each paralleled, challenged, and nurtured the other.

One expression of this creative matrix is romanticism. By placing the individual at the very center of life and insisting that it is the power of imagination that gives meaning to that life, the romantic vision introduces the quest for reunion with the idealized figure of the "other self."

This ethereal perspective could not remain "pure" very long in an atmosphere of gradually emerging appreciation of the complexity of the human mind and growing understanding of the emotional turbulence within each person.

This early romantic imagination was transformed by the Enlightenment's lively questioning of authority and its natural scientific attention to everyday experience. One expression of this more mundane outlook was a newly developing literary form bent on offering realistic representation of the soiled world of common people. Out of the dark night of the irrational, the romantic brew was poured into the contrastingly crude container of the novel's adherence to the ordinary and the everyday. Subjected to such a catalytic cauldron, this already unstable mix became violently volatile.

Unable to form a reconciling compound, the opposing elements of darkness and light produced instead an ambivalent archetype of contemporary alienation. The Gothic villain is the original antihero. Divided against himself, he swings back and forth wildly between evil deed and penitent mood.

Although still a precursor to the literature of the Double, the eighteenth-century Gothic novel represented a clear beginning of explicitly acknowledged exploration of the divided self. Because it emerged prior to the recognition of the role of the unconscious, its villain-hero's war of impulse and remorse was that of a natural man (or woman) encountering the most marvelous/terrible supernatural forces.

The Gothic imagination was fascinated with the exploration of the irrational, but the dark impulses on which it focused were still too awful to yet be fully acknowledged as psychological processes wholly contained within the individual self. The external projections of the unconscious appeared in the metaphor of haunted medieval castles housing subterranean vaults laced with secret passages and trap doors through which ghosts and demons menaced the protagonist. In this way the Gothic novel was able to explore the division of self in the image of a realistically believable daylight character subjected to nightmarelike supernatural events.

As an expression of this interplay between probability and imagination, in 1796 Matthew Lewis wrote *The Monk*.[8] Although described by its author as "a romance," it serves as one of the transitional works that connect the tradition of the Gothic novel with the explicitly psychological nineteenth-century literature that it prefigured.

Instead of a haunted medieval castle, the setting is a Catholic

39

abbey at the time of the Inquisition. Catacombs replace sub-terranean dungeons, and supernatural figures out of religious folklore serve instead of ghosts. Written by Lewis when he was only twenty, this tale of war between the flesh and the soul reads like an elaborate adolescent sexual fantasy.

The monk, Ambrosio, appears at first as a man so holy that he spends every hour "in study, total seclusion from the world, and mortification of the flesh."[9] This one-sided severity of seeming purity is a disavowal of the other half of his humanity. It is the sort of spiritual pride that makes a person most vulnerable to the damning temptations that seem to come from outside of the self.

It is Ambrosio's arrogance that allows him to be seduced by Mathilda, the devil's agent, disguised as a novice. She enters the monastery. Using the unconscious force of the monk's own un-acknowledged passion, she overcomes his denials. Once seduced, Ambrosio inevitably gives way to an increasingly wicked life as he himself becomes a cruel exploiter and seducer of other innocents. Exploring every form of what was once unthinkable, he participates in sodomy, incest, rape, necrophilia, and whatever other opportunities are available to the dark part of his self that has emerged from the shadows to dominate his life.

Though intermittently tortured by guilt and shame, he has been so corrupted that he cannot renounce his evil ways. Para-lyzed by the exquisitely painful awareness of his self-conscious-ness, he can no longer connect will with action. In the end, his divided self leaves him vulnerable to being needlessly tricked by the devil once more. This time, he settles for a moment of seem-ing freedom. The price is an eternity of damnation.

NOTES, CHAPTER 3

1. I am using the term *collective shadow* to designate only that part of the self that is unacceptable to a primary group with which the individual identi-fies. This should not be confused with Jung's use of the term to designate comparable disavowals for as yet undiscovered aspects of what he calls "the collective unconscious" (an inherited reservoir of archetypes).

2. C. G. Jung, "Psychology and Religion," from *Psychological Reflections* in *Collected Works*, Vol. 11, ed. Jolande Jacoby (New York: Harper & Row, Torchbooks, 1961), p. 216.

3. M. Esther Harding, *The 'I' and the 'Not-I': A Study in the Development of Consciousness* (Princeton, N.J.: Princeton University Press, Bollingen Series LXXIX, 1965), p. 77.

4. Alan Watts, *The Two Hands of God: The Myths of Polarity* (Toronto, Can.: The Macmillan Co., Collier Books, 1963).

5. Otto Rank, *The Double: A Psychoanalytic Study*, trans. and ed., and with an introduction by Harry Tucker, Jr. (Chapel Hill: University of North Carolina Press, 1971); Robert Rogers, *A Psychoanalytic Study of the Double in Literature* (Detroit, Mich.: Wayne State University Press, 1970); Masao Miyoshi, *The Divided Self: A Perspective on the Literature of the Victorians* (New York: New York University Press, 1969); and C. F. Keppler, *The Literature of the Second Self* (Tucson: University of Arizona Press, 1972).

6. The literature of the Double reflects the sexism that dominates most cultural products. The protagonist is male almost throughout and the Double is usually female only when the second self represents the feminine aspect of the hero. My use of the male pronoun in this sequence reflects (but does not support) that bias.

7. Some theorists contend that consciousness as we know it did not exist in the earliest human beings, and that it only gradually developed over a period running well into recorded history. Cf. Eric Neumann, *The Origins and History of Consciousness* (Princeton, N.J.: Princeton University Press, Bollingen Series XLII, 1954), or Julian Jaynes, *The Origin of Consciousness in the Breakdown of the Bicameral Mind* (New York: Houghton Mifflin Co., 1977).

8. Matthew G. Lewis, *The Monk*. (New York: Avon Books, 1975).

9. Ibid., p. 9.

CHAPTER 4

Saints and Sinners

Although I can identify readily with the self-torture that must have characterized Lewis's own sexual turmoil, I am relieved to report that at least so far I have fared better than his Gothic villain-hero, Ambrosio. The atmosphere in which I grew up was only intended to control the expression of sexual impulses, not to eradicate them entirely.

Sex was rarely a topic for open discussion in my family. Still it always seemed to lurk menacingly in the background. I soon learned to participate in the family practice of keeping sex in its place. My parents studiously avoided introducing the subject except to condemn any young man who "got a girl in trouble." Disturbing newspaper accounts of sexual assault were used as undetailed evidence for why it was crucial not to get "so excited that you could go crazy." As an early adolescent, I learned that if I must fool around I was to do it outside of the neighborhood. I could sow my wild oats with some Gentile girl but nothing "funny" (i.e., perverse). When I was ready to get serious, it would be time to bring home a nice Jewish virgin. Together we would produce grandchildren.

The only problem was that my masturbatory fantasies could not be contained within the narrow boundaries set by my parents.

My unruly sexual impulses simply did not fit the confines of what they had defined as an acceptable self for a nice Jewish boy. During puberty and early adolescence, I often feared that I was going crazy. I was sure that one day my mad wishes would explode into irrevocably destructive acts of perversion. For a while, the only way I could ease my anxiety was by imagining that I was divided into separate and contradictory selves. I was desperate to find a way to choose the acceptable self and to dispose of the other's body so cleverly that no suspicions would be aroused.

I was less than sixteen when I accidentally discovered the Gothic instrument that would free me from the fiend within. While frantically browsing in the highly recommended shop of a dealer in secondhand forbidden books, I came upon a copy of *Psychopathia Sexualis.*[1] Subtitled *A Medico Forensic Study (with Especial Reference to the Antipathic Sexual Instinct)*, and authored by an impressively titled Dr. R. von Krafft-Ebing, Professor of Psychiatry and Nervous Diseases at the University of Vienna, this late nineteenth-century self-consciously "scientific" work promised to be the solution to the problems of my divided self. I had come upon an educationally acceptable piece of almost pure pornography.

The book was a diversified collection of case histories of terrible/marvelous acts of perversion committed by criminally insane sex fiends. Best of all, the crucial descriptions were in Latin. What a find for a guilt-laden, sex-crazed, sixteen-year-old boy who was fortunate enough not to understand a word of Latin!

It was during my long hours of secret study of these clinical categories of corruption that I first found my vocational calling. Once more I had surrendered the playfully Dionysian impulses of my psyche to domination by its Apollonian aspect. At sixteen, I decided that some day I would become a psychiatrist and cure these pathetic perverts. Dividing my tortured self into *I*, the doctor, and *they*, the patients, I could play scientific saint to their psychopathic sins. No need for a haunted medieval castle or a

43

devil-possessed abbey. Like Drs. Jekyll and Frankenstein, those other latter-day Gothic physicians, my chamber of horrors would be the clinic and the laboratory.

It was in my early twenties that, as part of an internship in clinical psychology, I went to work at a state hospital Building for the Criminally Insane in a program for the psychiatric treatment of sex offenders. Demonic devices were limited to straitjackets and electroshock machines. There were no dungeons, no dank, dark cells in which prisoners were left to rot. Instead, in this clinical sanctuary there were sterile "Quiet Rooms" that sometimes housed patients who needed "therapeutic isolation." When I entered this contemporary Gothic setting, my need to deny my own tumultuously unruly sexuality made it impossible for me to imagine myself in the place of any one of these patients. Instead, I remained completely out of touch with the terror such a clinical horror chamber would have otherwise evoked from a more complete human being.

In the service of maintaining the denial of these unacceptable parts of myself I had to be able to ignore all that we had in common. In my own mind, I lumped together all of the sex offenders into one category and all of us good doctors in another. Unconsciously intent on maintaining the bastion that separated the good guys from the bad guys, I paid little attention to the ways that people *within* each category were different from one another.

Under the supervision of a more experienced psychologist, I had come to learn how to do psychotherapy. First as an observer and later as an apprentice participant, I was to sit in on two newly forming therapy groups that would be meeting three times a week over a period of years. All of the prisoner/patients in each group were convicted sex offenders.

The first meetings began with group members in turn sharing self-serving confessions of their secret crimes. I was fascinated by their accounts of acts so perverse that I had to insist that they were totally alien to my own imagination. These patients made wonderful containers for ready projection of the burden of my

44

own denied secret fantasies. Unwilling to admit even to myself that I had any place there except in the position of the good doctor, I welcomed hearing the confessions that so clearly identified the patients as being completely other than me.

Everyone there already knew that this was a sex-offender treatment program. Rather than take the chance of letting the rest of us get to know him, each group member simply took on the identity of a particular category of offender. Each offered a mitigated, somehow justifiable confession of child molesting, rape, exhibitionism, aggressive homosexuality, incest, or the like. I readily accepted the mock sense of belonging, mutual trust, and respect that these men seemed so quickly to develop out of this apparent openness and sharing. Imagining the relief they must have found in at last being able to share their terrible, isolating secret lives, I felt moved by my belief that each isolate would come to know and accept the others and so could risk being known to them.

My supervisor had tried to help me to see past the homogenized vision of the patients that resulted from my need to make a primary distinction between myself and them. Unfortunately, soon after our meetings began, he was out sick. Arrogantly unwilling to distinguish between his seasoned perspective and my own naive outlook, I insisted on running the groups myself. During one of those meetings, the group members staged a fight. In retrospect, I believe that their intent was to instruct me painfully that we could not simply be divided into doctors and patients. I could not arbitrarily take the place of my supervisor, and they would not be reduced to interchangeable units.

The focus of the fight was Ross's accusing Red of having violated the confidentiality of the group:

"So what?" Red broke in. "What's the diff' who knows? You all made the papers when you got busted."

"Yeah, we made the papers," Ross threw back angrily. "That was enough to hurt us and to shame our families. Why should we go through it again? The other guys in the Building know we're in for sex crimes but they *don't* have to know any more than that."[2]

45

Up to that point their conflict over violation of their group boundaries seemed like confirmation of the power of the mutual respect and acceptance upon which I believed that identity had been built. But then to bolster his crumbling defenses Red went on the attack:

"Ah, you're just touchy because you're [in for being] a queer and these guys might want a piece of your ass."

"At least that's better than being a baby fucker," Ross spat at him.

"Cut that out. You just cut that out," Red answered, his face flushing. "I'm in for carnal knowledge of a minor. That's all."

"Baby fucker, baby fucker, baby fucker," Ross taunted. Some of the other men joined in the catcalling.[3]

Wanting so much to appear the competent good doctor, I had unquestioningly accepted their simulation of community. Solidifying my image of "them" allowed me to be the "me" my parents had defined as an acceptable self. Now it was turning out that beneath their seeming goodwill toward their assigned identity as perverts, each patient had a self of his own. Under the oppression of the collective shadow cast by the allegedly nonperverted community (of which I fancied myself a charter member), each of these men was reduced to basing his self-esteem on comparing his offense with that of some other group member. If he had to identify himself as a sex offender, at least he did not have to consider himself the lowest form of pervert.

Each of these men did what he could to maintain and display some vestige of his individual identity. These actions made it increasingly difficult for me to continue to view them as a single undifferentiated mass. As they began to emerge from under the collective shadow I had cast upon them, each of these patients posed the threat of recognition as a particular person no longer entirely different from myself.

The idealized self-image demanded by my own early childhood experiences had left no place for uncontrolled free-form sexuality. Nothing could have seemed safer for the preservation of that image than my coming upon projections of my disowned wantonness in the form of sex offenders who had been condemned and caged to await my curing them. But I had not anticipated the disturbing power of this encounter with my shadow.

The Double would not stay fixed in an undifferentiated mass that could be dismissed as not-I. Each of these men had an individual self with its own personally acceptable and unacceptable sides. The singularity of each man's particular personality resisted dismissal.

When I retreated behind the bastion of being the good doctor, the group members insisted on italicizing the differences between my supervisor and myself. They had discredited my hidden assumption that sex offenders were all the same, and would not tolerate my pretending that therapists were interchangeable good guys.

First by staging their fight when my supervisor was out sick, they quickly undid my efforts to obscure the differences in competence between the novice and the seasoned therapist. For fear that the whole program would fold, I had been reduced to dropping Red from the group.

When the older therapist returned, he heard me out, shook his head slowly with the closed eyes and wry smile of a father faced with the mess made by a loved son trying too soon to play at being daddy. The other patients did not seem surprised when the older therapist had Red rejoin the group. It was a while before they talked over what they had been up to, and even longer before I was able to understand how I had invited the confrontation.[4]

Next they understood the differences between my character and my supervisor's, instructing me on the multiplicity of their meaning along the way. Most people would have described me as the more aggressive of the two, and my supervisor as the more globally passive sort of person.

The two groups in which we conducted cotherapy also differed in important ways. One group was more analytical, intellectualized, and verbal in its approach to problem solving. The members of that first group had no prior institutionalization, no history of nonsexual offenses, and presented an overall picture of social conformity. In contrast, the other group engaged in a good deal of antisocial acting out (including fist fights and open homosexual banter during treatment sessions). Most of the members of this second group had been incarcerated in the past and had a history of nonsexual offenses and/or of alcoholism.

Although my supervisor and I did not intentionally take different roles, each group interpreted our characteristic attitudes differently. The first group characterized me as the "hatchet man" who made them uncomfortable by my "tough confrontations and probing interpretations," while describing my supervisor as a "nicer guy" who helped by offering "support and understanding." Despite how they had intimidated me with their staged fight, the second group admired me as "a guy who talks up and gets things done" while often denigrating my supervisor as a "deadhead."

These repeated meetings with my shadow made it difficult to maintain my self-idealizations. In the person of these sex offenders, my Double had begun to make me disturbingly aware that the world could not be nicely divided into one homogenized group of bad perverts and another of good doctors. It was becoming increasingly difficult to submerge awareness of the inconsistent, irrational aspects of my disturbingly divided self.

In desperation, I pulled my mask on tighter. Ignoring my contradictory experiences as best I could, I spent more time daydreaming about the wonderfulness of my becoming an admired expert, a recognized, perhaps a renowned healer. I loved the deference I received from the custodial staff. They seemed to understand what a good doctor I was becoming and to appreciate the therapeutic value of what I was trying to do. We traded off. They let me know how important I was. In return, I acknowledged the significance of their efforts in the success of the treatment program.

Then one day I made the mistake of showing up before the masquerade was in progress. Curious to observe my patients outside of the group therapy setting, unnoticed I drifted down to the maximum security yard. As I stood quietly in a darkened doorway at one side of the yard, one of my favorite attendants emerged from another doorway on the far side. I realized that he was there to round up the group for the session that was to begin in a few minutes.

My patients constituted a small minority in this Building for the Criminally Insane. Most of the other inmates had not been sentenced under the State Psychiatric Sex Offender Statute. Many were dangerous combinations of madness and meanness.

For the first time it occurred to me that my favorite and most admiring attendant was faced with a problem. I wondered just how he would summon the patients privileged to participate in my psychotherapy group. He appreciated what a delicate problem this situation posed.

What sort of sensitive solution might he provide? The last thing I expected was to see him cup his hands into a makeshift megaphone through which he shouted hoarsely, "OK, you punks out there! Time for Kopp's Cocksucker Class!"

NOTES, CHAPTER 4

1. R. von Krafft-Ebing, *Psychopathia Sexualis (with Especial Reference to the Antipathic Sexual Instinct: A Medico-Forensic Study)* (New York: F. J. Rebman, Medical Art Agency, n.d.). The only authorized English adaptation of the 12th German edition.

2. Sheldon B. Kopp, *The Hanged Man: Psychotherapy and the Forces of Darkness* (Palo Alto, Calif.: Science and Behavior Books, Inc., 1974), p. 81. The entire incident is described on pp. 75-82.

3. Ibid., p. 81.

4. Ibid., pp. 81–82.

PART II

Severed Selves

Two selves distinct that cannot join again;
One stood apart and knew but could not stir,

. . . .

And as she came more near
My soul grew mad with fear.

> —James Thomson,
> "The City of Dreadful Night"

CHAPTER 5

Double Trouble

During those long years in the Building for the Criminally Insane, I found it increasingly difficult to maintain the illusion that I was entirely one sort of person and my patients another. It was true enough that these men had acted out publicly what I had only secretly fantasized, but they had not been locked up simply because they had unusual sexual appetites. Their "perverse acts" of exhibitionism, incest, rape, child molesting, and aggressive homosexuality had a common criminal denominator. What made these acts punishable offenses was not the aggressor's deviant sexuality, but the violation of the victim's civil rights.

In every case the victim was sexually intruded upon without his or her consent.[1] The fact that my patients had been assaultive and I had not clearly meant that we had different *forms* for dealing with our inner turmoil. I was repeatedly upset to learn how often the *contents* were the same.

My patients would not allow me to use them as passive containers for the parts of myself I needed to deny and discard. Slowly I came to understand that my own sexuality was as "deviant" as theirs. It took longer to recognize the subtle unpunished ways in which I too violated other people's sacred selves.

There is no way that I can compare my own brief voluntary visits with the agonizingly extended incarceration that my patients were forced to endure. I can only hope that they learned something useful from their contact with me. There seems no way that the therapy I offered them in that correctional/psychiatric chamber of horrors could have been as valuable to them as their instruction has been for me.

The Gothic setting for my early exploration of *the divided self* has its literary parallels. It was in the eighteenth-century Gothic novel that this psychological territory was first explicitly acknowledged. Later writers went on to chart the terrain. The nineteenth century was an especially uneasy time of self-division focused on conflicts between propriety and passion, art and life, manners and morals, and particularly between the rational and the irrational. As an attempted literary solution to what is simultaneously a personal and social problem, there emerged the ambiguous figure of the Double.

Over the last two hundred years, many serious writers have undertaken the exploration of the divided personality, but none more devotedly than Dostoevsky. Obsessed with the dualism of the human soul, again and again he wrote of the insoluble conflicts within each of us. Informed by his own personal anguish, his tales reveal a depth of understanding of the relationship between imagination and needless suffering as yet unmatched by contemporary psychology and psychiatry.

Dostoevsky spent a literary lifetime exploring and clarifying the oppositions between the conscious and the unconscious self, and between reality and the power of dreams, hallucinations, and imagination. His second book is his opening pronouncement of the obsession with the divided self that would mark so much of his later literary achievement. This first, flawed attempt is a novella titled simply *The Double*[2] (1846). Later he himself wrote that "the idea of it was . . . more serious than anything else which I have carried out in literature, but," he went on, "I utterly failed with the form of the story."[3]

Though there are points at which the writing drags, for me *The Double* remains a disturbingly engaging experience. This less widely read work was the prefiguration of so much of his later writing. It also offers a model for one of the basic modes used by others who have contributed to the literature of the Double.

The unfortunate antihero of Dostoevsky's story is a defensively timid, manipulatively ingratiating, weak and petty bureaucratic clerk named Golyadkin. His Double (Golyadkin II or Golyadkin Junior) is a bold and successful man of action.

The "real" Golyadkin is a failure whose triumphs occur only in fantasy. His Double's unlimited confidence is realized in practical social and career advancements. But the Double is not simply an idealized wish-fulfilling Walter Mitty compensation for the real Golyadkin's deficiencies.

Each in his own way is a ruthless power seeker. Irascible, truculent, and rebellious, Golyadkin Junior is more open in his vicious, callously self-centered deceitfulness. He is the more effectual of the two because, unlike his servile toady original, the Double does not need to convince himself that he is basically a good and humble civil servant.

Golyadkin Senior is a chronic worrier. In his perfectionistic attempts to eliminate the contradictions within himself, he obsesses endlessly, undoing each thought or impulse with another. If he is to maintain the illusion that he is in control of his life, he dare not overlook any possibility. Ironically it is just these anxious preoccupations that consume the energy he needs to cope with the pressures of his personal life and his career.

Pretending that things are better than they are, he makes his situation worse than it is. He adds to his troubles by denying his complicity in the never-ending stickiness of his dishonest efforts at getting along with other people. He stubbornly insists that he is ever again on the verge of a new and better life. At the same time his denial of responsibility for what he does leaves him less and less in charge of himself, more and more likely to fail to improve his situation.

As the story begins, we find Golyadkin at home early one morning already devoted to stubbornly unwitting preparation of all the minor catastrophes he will be so surprised to encounter later in the day. He should be going off to his job as a government office clerk. Instead he is immersed in pretentiously dressing himself with all the elegance appropriate to the special person he insists on imagining himself to be.

The conscious goal of this particular morning's efforts is to make a good impression at a dinner party to which he is sure he has been invited. The party is to be held at the home of an important government official. Though the older man is hardly aware of the existence of this insignificant clerk, Golyadkin sees him as his mentor. Fantasies about his own imagined importance to the official extend beyond career advantages and on to marrying the older man's daughter, with whom he believes himself to be in love.

A series of chance encounters along the way to the dinner party further establish Golyadkin's character. Riding in a hired carriage, he first passes two young co-workers from his office. It is an awkwardly self-conscious moment for Golyadkin. Disowning his embarrassment, he misperceives them as ridiculing him. It is clear that his projection of this self-criticism makes him peculiarly irritable in ways that isolate him and invite ridicule.

A little later Golyadkin's hired carriage passes his department head's elegant coach. Obviously the boss is surprised to come across this clerk whom he had assumed to be hard at work in the office. Equally unprepared for this second encounter, Golyadkin is flooded with the sort of self-tormenting doubts that chronically emerge to obscure awareness of the fundamental contradictions in his nature. Unable to tolerate his seemingly unanswerable questions about *who he is to be*, he displaces his conflicts to safer issues concerning *what he is to do*.

In a moment he is lost in his ruminations. Each idea or impulse is obsessively balanced and undone by the succeeding force of its opposite:

Shall I bow? Shall I make some response? Shall I admit it's me or shan't I? . . . Or shall I pretend it's not me, but someone extraordinarily like me, and just look as if nothing had happened? It really isn't me, it *isn't* me, and that's all there is to it. . . .[4]

Raising his hat to the department head, Golyadkin finally says nothing. Once the opportunity to speak has passed he immediately regrets his inaction.

Dostoevsky's grotesquely deadpan humor reveals Golyadkin struggling with his own foolishness while blaming others for forcing him to behave badly. The clerk's next stop is at the office of a physician with whom he presumes he has a much more intimate relationship than actually exists. Once inside the doctor's consulting room, the clerk describes his entire painfully embarrassing situation. His is the life of an innocent victim of vague persecution and undefined slander. The doctor feels put upon by Golyadkin's insistently confidential sharing of sulky complaints about not getting the promotion he seeks and not developing the love relationship he wants. Others are blamed. The role of his own passivity and stubbornly wishful thinking are ignored.

After all of these needlessly anguished encounters along the way, at last Golyadkin arrives at the home of the official whose dinner party he expects to attend. There he is humiliated to learn that he has *not* been invited and that he will not be admitted. Reluctantly the clerk leaves, all the while making up excuses that allow him to deny whatever threatens to contradict his idealized vision of himself. As a result, by his own peculiar standards, he is able to justify later returning to intrude upon the celebration to which he had never been invited. Awkward and out of place, he ends up defending his stumbling, bumbling behavior until he has to be thrown out bodily.

That stormy night, Golyadkin rushes aimlessly along the deserted streets. Frantically fleeing, he has the look of a man wishing to hide and escape not only from his enemies, but also from himself. Just then, he has his first momentary encounter with the disturbingly familiar figure of the Double: ". . . he thought that someone had just been standing right there beside him . . . had even spoken to him—had spoken quickly, jerkily and not altogether intelligibly, but had said something of intimate concern to him."[5]

Shaken by the near meeting, Golyadkin quickly turns away

from this opportunity to see his life in a new perspective. Willing to explain away the experience as a dream, a moment's madness, or a mistake, he returns his attention to "justifying himself in his own eyes by various irrefutable arguments, and so salving his conscience completely."[6] It was not so much a matter of unwillingness to change his mind. Rather it was intolerance of recognizing that what he posed as his personal absolute reality was no more than a particular relative subjectivity, far less reasonable or consistent than he might have wished. As usual, "uneasiness and uncertainty about something that touched him intimately always tormented him more than the thing itself."[7]

Again and again, Golyadkin encounters this stranger who seems to know all about him. At first he is unable to avoid these disturbing meetings. Soon he begins to look forward to them. Eventually it is Golyadkin who pursues the stranger, until one day he follows him to the clerk's own home. The stranger not only seems to know his way, but is admitted by Golyadkin's servant as though he were the master. When Golyadkin I finally confronts Golyadkin II comfortably at home in his apartment, he can no longer deny that this stranger is a double of himself.

With characteristic indirectness, Golyadkin I tries to put off the Double with politeness, to overcome him with meekness. While the other looks and dresses the same as the original, this reflection is as openly aggressive as the first is hypocritically compliant. The result is a relationship in which the Double easily takes over, boldly making the clerk look more and more the fool while crowding him out of whatever place he holds at work and in his love life.

The mischievous Double does not restrict his areas of interference to Golyadkin's career and courtship. His scandalous behavior ranges from outrage to impropriety. There is, for example, a scene in a café in which Golyadkin has eaten a single pastry. He finds himself presented with a bill for eleven. The extra ten pastries have been eaten by his Double, who has slipped away without paying. The upright, well-intentioned Golyadkin is disgraced mostly by having the other side of his idealized conscious self revealed.

Mired in moments of indecision and revision, Golyadkin's long-delayed public challenge of the imposter's position comes too late. His counterfeit possesses all the self-assurance and aggressive social competence that he has disowned. When Golyadkin finally attempts to reclaim his place, he finds that the other has completely discredited him. No one will believe him. The pretender has convinced everyone that the "real" clerk is a madman. Irrevocably displaced by his Double, Golyadkin is hauled off to an insane asylum.

Dostoevsky's grotesquely ironic turnabout ending has probably contributed to those popular psychological/literary interpretations that reduce this disturbing novella to no more than an interesting account of the psychotic breakdown of a paranoid personality. Just as Golyadkin tries to discount the Double as a crazy notion, an error, or a dream, critics have often attempted to limit the personal impact of this shadowy figure by assigning it the status of a hallucination or a pathological aspect of a multiple personality syndrome.

The psychiatric diagnosing of Golyadkin and his Double allows the reader reassuringly protective distance from discomforting awareness of too personal an identification with the divided life of this self-deceptive character. By disowning the Golyadkin in ourselves, we can deny how often we too are not all that we believe we should be. Secretly we know that our hidden desires are irrational and our motives impure. Maintaining our idealized self-images sometimes requires our setting aside as inappropriate urges too earthy to be openly expressed, too savage to be even privately fantasized.

In each of us a good deal of psychic energy is consumed in maintaining the bastion needed to contain the parts of ourselves that we have learned to disavow. The more rigidly divided any of us is, the more compulsive the vigilance required to ward off the threat of losing control. This exaggerated posture of defense by one part of the self against another may be seen in any of us from time to time.

The extent of this division depends on our upbringing. All children begin in a natural, un-self-conscious state of spontaneity.

59

Bodily tensions and frustration are not tolerated. Those under the infant's control (such as urination and bowel movement) are immediately relieved. Tensions that the child cannot relieve on his or her own (such as hunger) are signaled by outcry that begins as a simple expression of discomfort and soon becomes a means for soliciting mother's care in alleviating that discomfort. Gradually the range of spontaneous behaviors for relieving instinctual tensions is extended beyond these simple primitive bodily functions. For a long while very young children continue to act on impulse much of the time. They simply do what they do without stopping to evaluate what they are doing, or what it means about who they are, or what they are worth.

Out of some amalgam of personality and cultural background, parents and significant others soon interrupt this natural spontaneity. Their reactions begin to shape a child's behavior, attitudes, and sense of self-worth. Praise and rewards may be offered for "good" behavior. Punishment or angry threats may be meted out for transgressions. Disapproval and contempt may be expressed if the child fails to live up to parental expectations.

Acceptance and praise foster a feeling of well-being in the child. They encourage confidence, spontaneity, and a sense of being worthwhile. Punishment and threat induce guilt feelings, moralistic self-restriction, and pressure to atone. Guilt is the anxiety that accompanies transgressions, carrying with it the feelings of having done bad things and the fear of parents' angry retaliation.

In the interests of self-protection, the child learns to deal preemptively with this anticipated punishment by turning it into the internalized threat of a sense of guilt. If the expected punishment is sufficiently harsh as to seem unbearably painful, threatening mutilation or destruction, the child may go beyond constraining the impulse and feeling guilty about it. When guilt evokes sufficient anxiety, the child will have to repress even the thought of having such an impulse. Whole segments of the self may have to be so totally denied, discredited, and disowned, that those of us whose painful childhood experiences encouraged

such radical disavowal of instinctual impulses become caricatures of self-control. Our defensive intellectualizations, stiff body
posture, and stilted social manner combine to make us seem like
windup toys driven to persist in courses of action already clearly
irrelevant or even absurd.

All the while we insist on thinking of our actions and attitudes
as "reasonable." It is more than obvious to those about us just
how dogmatic, stubbornly opinionated, and pedantic we really
are. It's not that we are openly argumentative or disagreeable.
Instead, by concentrating attention on irrelevant details, we ignore the personal aspect of our exchanges with other people.
Rightly enough, they experience the veiled criticism implicit in
our seemingly reasonable postures.

Our natural impulses are unavailable and our feelings are
constrained. We are not likely to have much fun. Nor are we
likely to *be* much fun. Our studied, effortful self-conscious manner
leaves little space for lightness or spontaneity. If not altogether
humorless, we confine our wit to dry or cutting comments. Dig-
nified and deliberate, we experience our own simplest wishes
for ease and pleasure as temptations that must be avoided or
ignored. We try our best to behave as we should. We dare
not do just as we please. We might lose control, or even go
crazy. Then everything could fall apart.

Unfortunately, our self-control is limited to saying no to our
impulses. Paradoxically, the more we insist on maintaining the
illusion of mastery, the less in charge of our lives we find ourselves. Tidying up the details of an ultimately unmanageable
life is an endlessly exasperating effort. Whatever energy remains we invest in attempts to parallel our external ordering
with an illusion of inner certainty. We imagine that if only
we carefully considered every alternative, then we could be
sure that everything would turn out perfectly.

This impossible chore adds an element of reassuring reluctance and procrastination to our every action. We add to our
indecisiveness by attempting to resolve unanswerable questions. What is reasonable, fair, normal, and right? we ask.

61

Unrelenting ruminations and abstract worries can serve to keep us out of more active trouble. Pondering the profundities of the role of aggression in the survival of the species, we are unlikely to bother with the pettiness of expressing momentary anger in a personal confrontation. At times these abstract, idealized distractions offer the reassuring illusion that we are above the muddle of everyday irritations and disappointments. Ultimately, insistence on unattainable goals of complete mastery and perfect order takes us back full circle. Again and again we are threatened with awareness of the unresolvable contradictions in our selves.

Our immediate reaction is to become anxious about losing control. We seek even greater distance from our unacceptable emotional aspect. Even when things are going well, obsessional characters tend to think elaborately rather than simply feel.

Ordinarily, thinking about feeling is enough to dampen passion. Under pressure, this detachment may have to be escalated into the rather desperate refinement of confining attention to thinking only about thinking. Even that more elegant defensive maneuver may prove insufficient for totally suppressing the tumultuous emotional life that we are attempting to disown.

Desperate times call for desperate measures. It is then that generalized character style may have to be supplemented by particularized neurotic symptoms. Failing efforts to avoid uncontrolled feelings may be supported by draining away escaping energy and excitement into a morass of debilitating depression. Increased security efforts may be justified by the proliferation of irrational fears that require still further restriction of opportunities for unexpected experiences. Or we may immerse ourselves in isolating addictions that quiet our secret longings without acknowledging the emotional hunger they represent.

It is possible to maintain this division of self into conscious thought and ignored emotion, but the cost is exorbitant. Avoiding risky impulsive actions requires an unlived life of protracted procrastination, each move dogged by doubt and indecision. The compulsive search for perfect order leaves us chronically critical of every experience. Nothing is good enough to warrant joy. Our own insufficiencies leave us ever expectant of criticism. We may hold ourselves detachedly aloof from hurt and humiliation, but we will have walled ourselves off from acceptance and tenderness as well.

Being bright and energetic does not help such people. If anything, compulsively misdirected intelligence simply serves to ensnare a person in more and more elegant emotional traps. That painful irony slowly became clear to an obsessional character whom I once treated. Martha had endured several years of depression while researching and analyzing all of the available literature on the advantages and disadvantages of undergoing psychotherapy.

In itself her questioning of the process was not unreasonable. Her approach to the problem was appropriate to her academic background. However, in the service of supporting the bastion against emotions, her research accomplished little more than to make her fearful procrastination seem sensible.

Martha did not get around to making her first appointment until she found that her work situation was "rapidly deteriorating." For several years she had managed well as a university administrator. Usually her "vocational self" could handle anything that it was asked to do. It did its best work under pressure.

But in recent months, the situation at the university had gotten worse and worse. The more committed her own efforts, the more irresponsible she found those of her colleagues, of her support staff, and particularly of her boss. Like her father, the university president sloughed off his own duties again and again, leaving her "stuck with cleaning up his mess."

Not that she cared any more what her aging father did or did not do. They had never been particularly interested in each other. He had always had more time for struggling with her rebellious older sister than for appreciating Martha's own efforts to be good. Father himself, she deplored, was a self-cen-

63

tered undependable wastrel, given to fits of temper when he did not get his own way.

The family home was halfway across the country. If not for her duty to mother, Martha would not even have bothered to continue her infrequent obligatory holiday visits. It was "super-mom" who had seen her through this childhood of paternal neglect. Not that mother was ever completely satisfied with anything or anyone, but she had often praised Martha for being a basically good and sensible little person. It was mother's encouraging Martha "to disdain petty pleasures and set aside self-pity" that had made possible the daughter's devotion to academic achievements.

Developing a divided self had been necessary for psychological survival in the difficult family situation in which Martha grew up. In the work world that had become the center of her adult life it had not served her as well. By the time she came to see me, she had begun to experience the bitterness of how unfair it all seemed. It was not only the burden of getting stuck with having to clean up after the boss's impulsive decisions. What was even more painful was finding herself left out of the personal exchanges shared by the other women on the administrative staff.

Sometimes she believed that she did not fit in because she served as the conscience of the department, sometimes because she was the only one who had neither husband nor lover. In any case, clearly it was unfair. The others seemed so selfish and frivolous, and yet they had both mutual acceptance and men who cared about them. She who worked so hard and gave so much of herself ended up excluded and alone.

At first I tried to establish a therapeutic alliance by empathically reflecting her feelings. She responded by backing off from what she experienced as my inviting her self-pity. She knew that she *should* not feel all that bad. After all, other people had it worse. Someone had to take responsibility for the hard part. She *ought* to be satisfied with knowing that she was doing the right thing. If there was more to it than that, she was *supposed* to figure it out on her own. Depending on other people would be both weak and hazardous.

Only gradually did she begin to recognize how much of this moralistic cant was a protective denial of hidden vulnerability and secret emotional pain. It was during this transformation that she reported the following dream:

I was walking along what seemed like a clean, safe, suburban street. There was something disturbingly unreal about it. Every house and every tree looked exactly the same. All at once, I realized that they were all just plastic cutouts. I began to run but I saw that the only way out was through a dark, ugly, dirty old door at the dead end of the street. It was horrible. I was still upset when I woke up.

With her associations to that dream came conscious awareness of how frightened she was of losing control of her improper, confused, "selfish" feelings. She remembered how young she had been when she first decided that she was just not meant to have much of a "personal self." A life of work and sacrifice would have to be enough. As she began to realize how much more than this she wanted, Martha felt ashamed.

Coming to accept and pursue her longings took time, trust, and many tears. Piece by piece she replaced her immutable rules for right living with more flexible guidelines. Learning to settle for more imperfect order and less controllable happiness required paying more attention to her feelings and practicing more effective emotional expression.

Though increasingly more self-assertive and independent, she discovered she might still wish to limit doing just as she pleased sometimes. It turned out that this prim and proper workaholic had been engaged in a secret struggle. Beyond the dream door was the fantasy that she would quit her job, "buy a string bikini, go off to the beach at Acapulco, and fuck everything in sight." Her new constraints arose out of realistic consideration for others and concern for practical consequences rather than out of some abstract feeling that she was not supposed to be "selfish." Martha still had problems, and some conflicts remained difficult to resolve. Still, more and more of the time, she felt that it was all right to be on her own side. Life had not become easy, but it sure felt easier.

A self obsessively divided between obligation and abandon is always a maintenance problem. Martha's unacceptable feelings and disowned longings were widely projected onto almost everyone whom she encountered. Images of her Double caught her eye in every sliver of that shattered mirror. In her bewilderingly fragmented world only her narrowly focused sense of duty remained intact. Everyone else seemed selfish and irresponsible. Paradoxically, the same life that repaid her own devotion with deprivation rewarded these underserving self-seekers.

It was different with Max. Like Martha, he too had a self divided between italicized high ideals and bracketed base motives. He too chose thought over feeling and put principle above desire. His frantic efforts to be certain that he was right required the comprehensive consideration of every alternative. This search for perfect certainty usually paralyzed any prospect for action.

Unlike Martha, Max had narrowly fixed the projection of his own double onto a particular aspect of archetypal abandon. Max spent his late adolescence and early adulthood pursuing the elusive shadowy figure of the drunken woman.

Among the many problems cited as his reasons for seeking psychotherapy was the "mildly embarrassing" fact that at age twenty-four, Max was still a virgin. Though he had met several young women whom he found attractive, somehow he never had gotten around to asking any of them to go out with him. Gratuitously, he assured me that his reluctance was *not* a problem of personal shyness. Again and again he explained that it was simply an expression of his criticism of a culture that imposed "inequitable gender-linked role differentials."[8]

At the time I was a young, unseasoned therapist. I still believed that facts could change attitudes. Spitting into the wind, I pointed out that despite these complex role differentials, lots of other young men seemed to be getting laid.

It was then that Max told me of his pubescent fantasy that he would someday encounter a drunken woman. Her "alcohol-in-duced disinhibition and wantonness" would render her as eager as he for their sexual union. For years, whenever he saw a woman on the street whom he imagined might be drunk, he would follow her for blocks and blocks. I don't know whether or not any of these women he hounded were really drunk. In every instance, just about when it was time to accost his Double, Max would decide that he had been mistaken, that the woman was not drunk at all.

After we had been meeting for therapy twice a week for several months, Max happened upon an attractive young woman who seemed to fulfill his requirements in an unexpected way. Though she did not drink, she appeared to have "a culture-free sexual frame of reference." Only moments after they met she discarded the traditional role differential by letting Max know that she found him exciting, wanted to be alone with him, and most remarkable of all, she wanted to go to bed with him.

They met at work on a Monday. Her family was to be out of town on the following Friday. She gave Max her address and asked him to come to her house the night that her folks were to be away. She promised that she and Max would make love.

Between their first meeting and his appointed deflowering, Max came in for his regular Thursday morning appointment. He told me of his good fortune and of his nervously excited anti-cipation of his "moment of sexual fulfillment." Though his obsessional doubts and unanswerable questions resurfaced inter-mittently to deflect his thrust toward action, he left the session undaunted.

When next we met on the Monday morning following what was to have been his long-awaited transition rite, Max looked more daunted than fulfilled. But as he began to bring me up to date about his adventure, his earlier excitement returned. How long he had awaited an opportunity like the one offered by this young woman. For the first time, he was not the one who had to do the asking. At last he could be sure that he was as much wanted as wanting. She had done the courting. This had been his one great chance for sexual union without risk of rejection.

Although she lived in an unfamiliar neighborhood, he was not for a moment distracted by his usual searching of strange streets for the sight of some drunken woman. He made straight for the home of this bold young woman who would open the door to his new life of sexual adventure. Leaping the porch steps at a single bound, Max made the mistake of pausing before the door to consider his situation.

About to knock, for just one moment he insisted on thinking over what he was about to do. Through that crack in his resolve, familiar doubts rushed in to save him from losing control of his feelings. He wondered whether or not he could really be sure that what he thought he was trying to do was what he was supposed to want to do. Soon he stood paralyzed by his self-consciousness.

Then all at once it came to him. Suddenly he realized that *it was a Friday!* "Wouldn't you just know it? The one time I find a woman who is so free of the inequitable role differential that *she* asks *me* to make love, and of course it turns out to be Friday! Friday, the day our Lord died for our sins. The Savior laid down his life for my sake. How could I have even thought of indulging my sexuality on the very day that He chose to sacrifice Himself?"

Meeting with this woman provided Max an opportunity for self-acceptance. Unfortunately, he was not yet ready at the time. This intimacy with his Double could have allowed his laying claim to the disowned urgency of his instincts. Instead Max's anxiety turned him toward a frantic search for "higher" principles. The result was a lunatic reinstatement of his false self.

As his therapist, I thought it seemed promising that even momentarily he could be so vulnerable to experiencing his own sexuality. He came so close to overcoming the bastion of his divided personality that he had to call in the calvary.

Paradoxically, it was his lunatic evocation of this inflated ego-ideal that allowed Max to begin to recognize just how irrational his "rational" ruminations could be.

Eventually, he was able to understand the needless self-sacrifice of his imitation of Christ. Slowly and painfully, he was able to reclaim some of the inner fire and longing that he had so long ago renounced. More and more, he was able to choose the antic pleasure of a life that combined the seeming contradictions of self-discipline and self-indulgence, systematic thought and irrational feeling, reasonable caution and exciting adventure. Though filled with contradictions, this acceptance of the eternal oppositions within himself was far more fun than the controlled consistency of the sober pursuit of his drunken Double.

NOTES, CHAPTER 5

1. In some cases, the victims were too young to give knowledgeable consent.
2. Fyodor Dostoevsky, "The Double," in *The Great Short Works of Fyodor Dostoevsky*, with an introduction by Ronald Hingley (New York: Harper & Row, 1968), pp. 1–144.
3. Ibid., quoted in Hingley's introduction, p. ix.
4. Ibid., pp. 7–8.
5. Ibid., p. 39.
6. Ibid., p. 46.
7. Ibid., p. 47.
8. After a while I came to understand that this translated to mean approximately: "It's just not fair that the guy should always be the one who has to ask the gal for the date and risk being turned down." Unfortunately, Max had come of age too early to benefit from the recent shift in relationships brought about by the "new morality" and by the impact of the feminist movement.

CHAPTER 6

A Self of One's Own

Parents who remain out of touch with their own upsettingly passionate natures may burden their children with similarly excessive controls. Like Martha and Max, these selectively damaged children grow up having well-defined but divided selves. Even so their repressed wishes cannot be made to disappear completely. However indirect and distorted their expression, the shadow sides of their personalities will not be denied.

Dostoevsky dramatized how consciously discarded impulses and feelings are unconsciously projected onto the Double. Fantasy and reality are so intricately intertwined that at times Golyadkin II appears to be an actual person. Other times he seems an almost hallucinatory phantom of the original clerk's imagination. Only one thing is clear throughout. Golyadkin I is least prepared to confront in his Double just those attributes that he himself publicly disdains and secretly envies.

From time to time, each of us has trouble comfortably encompassing the opposing forces that comprise our own inevitably contradictory natures. In the obsessive-compulsive neurotics there is an exaggerated horizontal split between their acceptably civilized surface selves and underlying disruptively primitive private passions. For a time their parents were appropriately accepting of the child's earliest infantile needs. Once the child got a bit older, one or both parents unexpectedly changed into selectively harsh tamers of whichever impulses made them too anxious. They could not permit these wild ways. As grown-ups, such children turn out to be detached, overcontrolled characters given more to ruminative thought than to passionate feelings and preferring picky procrastination to bold action.

Despite these characterological limitations, the *neurotic personality* is the least damaged of the psychopathologically divided selves. Though it can be difficult and costly to maintain its horizontal division of repression, compared with that of other divided selves neurotic suffering is more selective and contained.

In the childhood of the neurotic personality, the overly severe parental injunctions against the expression of particular instinctual urges came late enough to first allow the development of a cohesive self. When parental insensitivity and abuse of the infant occur during the earliest months of life, the result can be a shattering of the beginning self so total that what is left is a *psychotic personality*.[1]

Those children who are damaged later and less severely during the first three years also suffer effects on the newly forming self. However, these *borderland personalities* get the chance to contrive a false self. This protects the poorly developed, still archaic core self from being shattered. The contrived false self represents the baby's giving up of its own needs in order to take care of the mother's needs. Such a solution is costly and can be hazardous, but as a survival technique it saves the child from going crazy or falling into a lifetime of wordless despair. Like the neurotic, the borderland personality suffers needlessly in the service of maintaining disavowal of unacceptable aspects of the self. However, unlike the neurotic, the borderland personality never had sufficient opportunity to evolve a dependably cohesive self at the outset, and as a result sustains more pervasive residuals of childhood damage.

Like the neurotic, the borderland personality also suffers needlessly in the service of maintaining a division of the self.

71

But the borderland personality has more at stake. The neurotic struggles against repressed urges that push for expression from beneath the idealized container of the seemingly civilized self. But the neurotic only risks punishment for a feared loss of control that would blow his or her cover. The borderland must manage to ignore a parallel archaic self that threatens the personality with "coming apart" to reveal itself as an empty fraud. Because of this, the borderland's efforts are largely devoted to seeking the repeated reassurance needed to maintain self-esteem. Little energy or attention is left over to discover just what is most wanted out of life, or how to go about getting it.

During the earliest years borderland personalities were treated impersonally. Attentive personal care that is responsive to a particular baby is needed to provide the safety, support, and freedom necessary for sound psychological growth. In the absence of sufficiently empathic mothering, children are unable to develop a solidly separate independent individual self. Lacking a clear sense of who they are as children, they grow into adults who remain vulnerable to feeling as though they lack a central core of personal identity. They have no clear sense of existing in their own terms. The question *Who am I?* remains a continually recurring focus of confusion in their lives. Again and again what has been defined as self can too easily become depleted, fragmented, even menaced by the threat of annihilation.

This uncertain sense of self in adults reflects parental intrusion and/or neglect during the earliest years. There are many ways in which any particular child may miss out on the personal care needed to develop a sound sense of self. Good enough mothering may be situationally in short supply in homes in which mother has too much else to do and too little support for her efforts. Institutionalized youngsters are almost certain to get short shrift from overworked, often poorly trained paid custodians.

Some children are deprived of good enough mothering by the unfortunate timing of parental illness. Suffering from physical pain, even the potentially best of mothers may lack the energy and concentration to give her baby the personal attention she would like it to have. Similarly, a mother who suffers an emotional depression during her child's infancy may have little vitality left over beyond that consumed by her private psychological distress.

The *reasons* for mother's inadequate care during the first three years of his or her life are of no consequence to the infant/toddler. Suffering neglect or intrusion, a child this young is not yet able to distinguish between the cruel abuse of an uncaring mother and the insufficient personal attention regretted by a loving but disabled one. The infant sees the mothering one as all-powerful and all-knowing. Consequently, each maternal act and omission is experienced as *intentional*.

Short periods of frustration need not have long-range psychologically damaging effects on the child's developing sense of self. As a matter of fact, some intermittent delay in the satisfaction of the baby's needs is crucial to its eventual separation from the feeling of being one with the mother. Good enough mothering requires parental ability and willingness to attend closely and attentively to the baby's moods and tensions. It also requires confidence in the child's capacity for autonomous development.

At times immediate gratification is needed. But the child must gradually develop a self adequate to dealing someday with a largely disinterested world. And so, one aspect of good enough mothering is helping the child build an increasing tolerance for frustration of immediate gratification of its needs.

Empathic mothering can be learned and practiced by those who care for children to whom they have not given birth. Foster or adoptive parents, day-care workers, and natural fathers can all develop good enough mothering skills. Clearly, some infants are easier to care for than others. Out-of-touch mothering may be the result of unrecognized or untreatable illness in the child. Sometimes, the mother's seeming lack of empathy is little more than an unfortunate mismatching of the infant's temperament and her own.

For those who lack a coherent, reliable, comfortably familiar sense of personal self, Dostoevsky's Golyadkin is not a fitting literary metaphor. Instead, borderland personalities are better able to identify with Kafka's Gregor Samsa. Boldly telescoping the interplay of fantasy and reality, in his long short story "The Metamorphosis"[2] Franz Kafka conveys the overwhelming intrusion of the unconscious on those unprotected by a consolidated personal identity:

As Gregor Samsa awoke one morning from uneasy dreams he found himself transformed in his bed into a gigantic insect. He was lying on his hard, as it were armor-plated, back and when he lifted his head a little he could see his dome-like brown belly divided into stiff arched segments on top of which the bed quilt could hardly keep in position and was about to slide off completely. His numerous legs, which were pitifully thin compared to the rest of his bulk, waved helplessly before his eyes.[3]

This grotesque transformation surrealistically dramatizes just how foreign Gregor finds his own inner being. His story has been interpreted from many different conceptual vantage points. It can be understood as the impact of disinterested socioeconomic system's claims on the anonymous individual. If so, the conflict is between what is expected of the impersonal "one" and what is needed by the personal self. From an existential point of view Gregor suffers from being born into a random world. Desperately he tries to project onto his life the appearance of order and meaning. But he discovers that the raw experience of his own personal being gives it the lie.

Within the context of depth psychology, Gregor's alienation from the core of his own personality is the result of living in a family in which no one knows who he is. No one tries to understand what it is like for him in particular. They all give the appearance of a concerned family. The illusion is so successfully maintained that no one recognizes that no one else cares.

In order to survive in this impersonal pretense of tenderness, unwittingly Gregor too has colluded in the deception. To protect himself against being flooded with overwhelming loneliness, he has had to go along with the others in ignoring his longing to be personally valued for himself alone. In settling for becoming what others expect him to be, he has sacrificed having a personal self of his own.

Gregor Samsa is a traveling salesman. Driven by his obligation to make money for the family, he spends much of his time alone and far from home. He loathes all of the impersonal aspects of his work, "traveling about day in, day out . . . worrying about train connections, the bed and irregular meals, casual acquaintances that are always new and never become intimate friends."[4]

He loathes the work but it is all he knows. In the service of his parents' expectations, it is what he has become. He works neither to get things for himself nor to pay off his own debts. Instead, he works only to pay back what his parents owe to others.

But it is not only Gregor's life that is empty of personal meaning. His parents' own identities are also curiously hollow. At times mother sounds caring, but she easily becomes no more than an anonymous echo of her authoritarian husband. This stubborn patriarch imagines he has power. That charade is maintained by the deceptive participation of the rest of the family. For example, they honor father's insistence on wearing his uniform at home as a way of pretending that he has not retired. During the family's after-dinner conversations, he always falls asleep. When his wife and daughter rouse him later to put him to bed, invariably he protests that he has been awake all the time. They offer mock respect, all the while attending him as though he were a big baby.

Everyone else in the family is chronically overworked and tired out. Though father himself does nothing, he claims all of the credit. Secretly he is as weak and as submissive as his son. Neither one knows who he really is. Mother acts as though she has no self of her own to assert.

Gregor has given years of his life to providing for his family. Though his parents demanded this, they never really needed it. Father had more money than Gregor knew. Mother passively participated in the deception.

In sacrificing his life to meeting his parents' self-absorbed expectations of him, Gregor discovers that his personal self has come to seem like a stranger. His transformation into a beetle is an expression of just how alien, incomprehensible, and even revolting his own inner being has become to him. Having lived most of his life as an impersonal false self, he fears that emergence of the real one can only lead to total annihilation. The shameful vermin he becomes makes terrifyingly clear that personal indifference has left him incapable of doing anything to ease his own loneliness. Living an unbearably empty life, longing for unattainable relief, at last he is reduced to nothing more than wishing to die.

The wordless depression and despair in the empty life of an adult often reflects something having gone terribly wrong in that earliest phase of childhood when the self was just beginning to develop. During the period when the infant must begin to contend with its separateness from the mother, it is most vulnerable to experiencing her inattention as abandonment and her interruptions as assault. The mother's face is the first mirror of that self the child is to become. The nature of her caretaking tells the child who it is. Looking into the mother's face, the baby sees responses that teach it to identify its own needs.

Unresponsive mothering eventually results in the child's own apathy about what could make it happy. Intrusive mothering may offer the baby no more than the irrelevant care that mother would like for herself. If this is all that is available, the baby may learn to accept it *as if* it were responsive to its own needs. Someday this child will be a grown-up who is always more attentive to what others want than to his or her own wishes.

Another common variant of not-good-enough mothering is that offered by an erratic mother who is interferingly attentive only when the baby's behavior makes her anxious. Her child will experience the world as dangerously unpredictable. Much of the energy that might have been invested in developing a happy adventuresome self will go into maintaining vigilance and control over a potentially harmful environment.

76

Whatever the variety of not-good-enough mothering, the child who misses out on those crucial months of empathic personal attention grows up uncertain about just who he or she is. If mother is too often out of touch with the child's needs, she will be experienced as dangerously undependable. When she does seriously disappoint the child, it will not feel safe to be angry at her.

There are parallel damaging attitudes that the child may also develop toward itself. It needs continuing experiences of being enjoyed for itself. Without these, later on it will not be able to be constructively self-critical. The feeling of being the all-bad baby will be threatened by destructive self-hatred as complete and dangerous as that felt toward the frustrating, seemingly all-bad mother.

What's a mother to do? She is supposed to frustrate her baby optimally for its own good. Even when both parents take responsibility for shaping the behavior of the emerging personality they are raising, there's no way to do it just right.

None of us can remember how we were mothered during those first preverbal months. Still, we may be able to reconstruct some of what that earliest care might have been like. We can begin by reviewing still-remembered later child-care experiences and considering how they make us feel about ourselves. Our best feeling will come from memories of times we felt lovingly accepted no matter what we had done.

Selective praise influenced our behavior without damaging our self-esteem. Threats of punishment also effectively determined how we behaved. Unfortunately, the guilt engendered sometimes resulted in repression of "bad" parts of our selves.

But reward and punishment are not the only ways by which family and community attempt to shape children's behavior. Among the traditional disciplines of child-rearing, it is *shaming* that is most damaging to the child's self-esteem.[5] The wholesale disapproval and contempt expressed in shaming can make the child feel totally unworthy. These later childhood experiences of shame evoke wordless echoes of forgotten earlier damage. Neglect and intrusion that occurred too early to be remembered will already have disrupted the baby's developing sense of self. Later shaming worsens the damage.

The total withdrawal of parental acceptance in both the earlier and later experiences implies the threat of abandonment or possibly of annihilation. If your parents don't appreciate you for who you are when you are a small child, you end up with a self that feels unacceptable. The experience can make you shy, avoidant, and ever anxious about making mistakes, appearing foolish, and being targeted for further ridicule.

Shaming usually takes the form of the parent expressing disappointment in the child by saying things like "Look how foolish you are, how clumsy, how stupid! What will other people think of you when they see that you can't seem to do anything right? You should be ashamed of yourself acting like that. If only you really cared, if only you wanted to act right, if only you tried harder, then you could be the kind of child we want you to be."

Repeated exposure to such abuse calls forth an inner echo of self-contempt. Eventually the child learns to say of itself, "What an idiot I am, what a fool, what an awful person! I never do anything right. I have no self-control. I just don't try hard enough. If I did, surely they would be satisfied."

The shaming parents are seen by the older child as good—or at least as well-meaning—loving people who might someday be pleased if only he or she were less imperfect. Like the infant intently watching the face of its self-absorbed mother, the child experiences itself mirrored in the parental disapproval. If it could conceptualize at that age, the baby might put it this way: "Mother is looking at me and what I see in her face must be a reflection of who I am."

To the older shamed child, it often seems no wonder that the parents are displeased and unhappy. My own mother often told me: "*I love you, but I don't like you.*" It was always clear that this meant she *loved* me because she was a good mother, but that she did not *like* me because I was an unsatisfactory child. Surely no one but my mother would have put up with me.

Even as an adult, for a long while recognizing my short-comings was equivalent to finding my self unacceptable. Human frailties are especially apparent in toddlers as they seek to develop independence and a sense of mastery of the world in which they live. As it should, each child's reach exceeds his or her grasp. There are many things that it wants to try at which it must first fail if it is ever to succeed. The experience of being seen as momentarily not yet able to cope is a natural part of growth. It is also natural to experience the embarrassment that accompanies stumbling, blundering, or making mistakes. To take on new activities, to develop skills, to be adventuresome, a child must risk the embarrassment of exposing itself unwisely and not well. At such times, the experienced loss of self-control is absolutely unavoidable.

If these inevitable embarrassments are not to turn into destructive experiences of shame, the parents must accept the child as he or she is. Some parents are too hard on their children because of their own personal problems, others because of harsh cultural standards. Some cultures make excessive demands for precocious maturing of the child. In such settings, shaming inculcates the feeling that other people will not like the child unless it lives up to their expectations.

When shaming arises out of the pathology of neurotic parents, the child is expected to take care of these self-absorbed adults. Such a child may never learn that the natural order of things is quite the reverse. He or she is discouraged from ever realizing that it is the parents who are supposed to take care of the child.

Even more insidious is the impact of the parent who unconsciously *needs* to have an unsatisfactory child. No matter how hard the child tries, or how much it accomplishes, such a parent will never be satisfied. Anything less than perfection is unacceptable. If the child gets a grade of 95 on an examination, it will be asked why it didn't get 100. If it gets 100, it will be asked what took it so long to get a satisfactory grade. Told that it should have been getting 100 all along, it may become afraid to do well lest perfect grades be demanded all the time from then on. If a chronic straight-A student, then the child may be asked, "If you're so damn smart, how come you can't keep your room clean?"

During this time of growing pursuit of mastery, it is especially important that parents back up the child's wish to stand on his or her own feet. Otherwise, the child may be overcome by a sense of shame at having exposed itself foolishly and prematurely.

A child is capable of enduring the inevitable embarrassments that attend occasional failures. It can still develop an autonomous sense of being a worthwhile sort of person. But this will *not* come about if the child is needlessly shamed into thinking that it should have been able to do those things that were simply too hard for it at the time.

Shaming parents express contempt and disgust for the child by ridiculing, by turning away, and by withdrawing their love. A child who is repeatedly treated in these damaging ways is pressured into feeling forever small, powerless, and unworthy. This can lead to spending a lifetime vainly seeking others' approval in the hope of someday having a self that has at last been validated.

NOTES, CHAPTER 6

1. Infantile autism, childhood schizophrenia, adolescent and adult chronic psychotic states are the catastrophic consequences of severe damage to the personality during this early phase of extreme vulnerability. In this book, discussion will be largely restricted to those of us who, though needlessly unhappy, are able to manage as functioning adults.

2. Franz Kafka, "The Metamorphosis," in *Selected Stories of Franz Kafka*, trans. Willa and Edwin Muir, with an introduction by Philip Rahv (New York: Modern Library, 1952), pp. 19–89.

3. Ibid., p. 19.

4. Ibid., p. 20.

5. Sheldon Kopp et al., *The Naked Therapist: A Collection of Embarrassments* (San Diego, Calif.: EDITS, 1976). An earlier, slightly different version of these explorations of shaming first appeared in this confessional anthology.

CHAPTER 7

Ashamed of Myself

Shaming played too large a part in my own upbringing. How is a small child to cope with continued discrediting of his or her evolving self? Imagining retaliation against "evil" parents is a poor substitute for realizing ways of protecting confidence in one's own self. Remaining excruciatingly sensitive to ridicule for much of my life, I have tried hard to avoid risking embarrassment. Pretending to be tougher than I was, I distracted attention from my own frailties by taking on the role of avenging angel. But no matter how I carried on, dramatized, and restricted my life, secretly I remained needlessly vulnerable to the catastrophic possibility of being exposed as a person who makes mistakes.

Embarrassment is always uncomfortable, but it need not be painfully destructive. Just as shame has long been misunderstood as being no more than a peculiar variant of guilt, so, too, the phenomenon of embarrassment has remained undifferentiated, as though it were no more than a low-keyed expression of shame. But shame is *not* guilt, and embarrassment is *not* shame.

Guilt is the anxiety about punishment that accompanies moral transgressions. *Shame* is the anxiety over disapproval that may come with failure to meet certain ego ideals.

Embarrassment, like shame, may accompany an experience of shortcomings. Unlike shame, embarrassment is rooted in situations of the moment, not in a person's overall appraisal of what he or she is worth as a human being. An act may seem unfitting without meaning that the total self is unacceptable.

Shame is a learned piece of *personal* pathology, a kind of needless suffering to which children do *not* have to be subjected. Those who have been shamed can some day learn to overcome feeling unworthy. Embarrassment is an inevitable natural reaction in certain *social* situations. No one is finally and completely safe from these predicaments of being caught off balance, but we can all learn to deal with such mishaps more creatively than we usually do.

The distress of embarrassment accompanies the experience of feeling unable to cope with some situation in the presence of others. The standard for how well we should be able to cope in any given setting depends on what sort of attributes and capacities we expect of ourselves as well as what we believe our audience expects of us.

Most often this potential crisis pivots on what kind of impression we believe we are making on the other people present in the social situation. It is of course possible to become embarrassed about what sort of a figure we *would* be cutting in the eyes of significant others who at the moment happen *not* to be present, just *as if* they were there. Nonetheless, the role of these fantasy figures is much more central in the occurrence of shame than in the embarrassment of a person who is merely feeling foolish for the moment.

Like shame, embarrassment has to do with unfulfilled expectations, but unlike shame, the expectations that are breached are *not* moral. The consequences may involve partial discrediting of social status. Some unexpected physical clumsiness, breach of etiquette, or interpersonal insensitivity may leave a person open to criticism for being cruder or coarser than he or she claims to be. But this is a matter of manners, *not* of morals. It may make for a temporary change of social status, but it need never carry the self-threatening sanctions of shame, with its implications of abandonment, loss of love, and ultimate emotional starvation.

Unfortunately, some of us have learned to believe that we should feel ashamed any time we turn out to be less than the perfect child our parents expected us to be. Making a mistake, doing something foolish, finding ourselves momentarily unable to cope, means that we are not worthwhile human beings. Instead of the momentary embarrassment inherent at times in being exposed as fallible, imperfect, merely human, we may experience overwhelming feelings of painfully degrading humiliation and disgrace.

All it takes for me (or for any of us) to be vulnerable to embarrassment is the unpleasant experience of being taken by surprise. This sometimes occurs even when receiving more of the good stuff of compliments and gifts than a person is prepared to handle.

These disruptions in my own life typically occur in the context of my going along implicitly trusting that I can take for granted my usual ability to make my way through the world. I assume that my mind and body will do their jobs well enough to meet the tasks at hand. I don't even consciously think about my faculties and their functioning. It's just me, doing what I do.

Then suddenly the unexpected occurs, something for which I am unprepared. I am caught unawares, especially if some particularly sensitive, intimate, or vulnerable aspect of myself is exposed. My taken-for-granted, natural, well-fitting behavior in the situation is instantly turned into inappropriate or incongrous fumbling. I become vividly aware of the discrepancy between the competently coping person whom I and others assumed I was, and the uncomfortably vulnerable fuck-up whose blunder is now exposed to my eyes and to theirs.

For a moment all bets are off. Trust of myself and others is in jeopardy. All values are once again in question. First there is the question of trust in myself. Am I an inadequate human being or a fool? What can I expect of myself? Do I really know what I am doing?"

Next comes the question of my trust in my assumptions about the other people who have witnessed this debacle. Trust is the focus especially when the embarrassment arises in the context of "the rejected gift, the joke or the phrase that does not come off, the misunderstood gesture . . . the expectation of response [that is] violated."[1] Will these people be kind or critical? Are they truly my friends? How do they really feel about me?

The sudden sense of exposure to others' seeing me as unable to deal with what is happening may leave me helplessly flustered. There is no way to avoid sometimes making mistakes, no way to be able to handle everything, no way to get it all just right.

This is the normal state of affairs. The natural reaction to the inability to cope in the presence of others is embarrassment. There seems to be no way for any of us to get through the day without making a careless error, doing something foolish, committing a faux pas. Every social encounter holds the risk of becoming embarrassing to one or more of its participants.

To the extent that the moment of embarrassment calls into question all trust in myself and others, it is potentially a dangerous time. It is then that I am most vulnerable to being flooded with shame as well, most open to transforming a momentary human blunder into a deadly discrediting of myself as a worthwhile human being. It is a time for the exotic flowering of my paranoia. At such times I may mistakenly expect contempt and ridicule from loving friends and neutral strangers. It is just as though they would turn from me in disgust as my parents did when I did not meet their impossible standards.

I remember an early instance of my own understandable embarrassment being escalated into shame by my mother's response. At the time I was about ten or eleven years old. Having insisted on wrapping me in swaddling as an infant, and having kept me under wraps as much as possible for many years, my parents took some time to be convinced to buy me roller skates. Because it might upset them, any adventuresomeness on my part was deemed inconsiderate. But somehow they had finally made space for my learning how to skate.

I behaved then as I still occasionally behave now. I punctuated my shyness and constraint with episodes of recklessness. That day I did it by taking off on my skates down a steep hill a city block long without being at all sure as to how I was to stop once I got to the bottom of such an incline. I went faster and faster, and I loved it. I was getting a little scared about how the trip would end when the lamppost on the corner caught my attention. I immediately envisioned myself making a grab for it and swinging around to a graceful vault.

I miscalculated. Rather than catching the lamppost in the crook of my arm I caught it full on one side of my face. The result was an incredibly painful and frightening collision, resulting in a super black eye and a torn muscle in my jaw.

After hitting the lamppost I sat on the curb and cried as little as possible. Now I was really worried. It was time to go home and face my mother. Instead of seeing this mishap as an unfortunate accident around which I could feel understandably sorry for myself and expect some sympathy, I knew that I had let my parents down again. Skates slung over my shoulder, I headed home and climbed the stairs to our apartment.

It was a summer day and the apartment door was open. I was careful to peer in with only one eye, shielding the battered side of my face from view. I called out loudly, "Ma, don't get upset. I got hurt but it'll be all right."

Only after warning her could I feel free to enter. Her response was completely predictable. "What now? Again you didn't stop to think about how much it would hurt a mother to see a boy who gets into so much trouble?"

I spent the next hour apologizing for my thoughtlessness, reassuring her that I would try to be a better boy. I consoled her in *her* grief at having such an inadequate son.

Now as an adult, after some therapy and much living, I am, for the most part, less vulnerable to shaming. Still, echoes of this grotesque situation can be heard at times from out of my unsettled and unworthy depths. I remember just a few years ago when I learned that I had to undergo a second bout of neurosurgery. In reality it was an unfortunate no-fault situation. Yet my first lunatic reaction was shame. For just a moment, all I could feel was, "Oh, shit! Now I've really made trouble for everybody."

Even after I had grown up, the problem was not entirely of my own making. People in our culture respond harshly to others' making mistakes in social situations. When an adult appears flustered, others often take it to be evidence of weakness, of low status, of immaturity, or of having something unenviable to hide. Understandably, when we blunder in the presence of others, we learn to try to conceal our inability to cope. Ironically, the blunderer often unwittingly reveals the discomfort of his predicament by the very means by which he tries to hide it: "the fixed smile, the nervous hollow laugh, the busy hands, the downward glance that conceals the expression of the eyes."[2]

This normal social need to conceal embarrassment is heightened in the person who has been excessively shamed as a child. Lack of self-acceptance requires developing a protective character style of acting timid most of the time and of usually avoiding letting others come to know you.

The result is a partially unlived life. A person who has been injured in this way simply cannot afford to risk participating in situations in which personal vulnerability might be revealed to others. Characteristically, people with a damaged sense of self assume that their own openness to the pain of ridicule is singular. They believe that other people are not as likely to appear foolish from time to time. Others are believed to be tougher and more competent than they.

This self-conscious preoccupation with being specially sensitive increases the sense of isolation, peculiarity, and loneliness. How sad that anyone must feel like a misfit, without knowing that ultimately we are all misfits. Basically we are not different from one another. None of us is able to cope every time with life's unexpected demands. The neurotically shy person's timid style is excessive in proportion to the belief that there is something specially wrong with him or her.

I do *not* mean to suggest that there is no such thing as normal shyness. The reserved manner of the introvert is probably part of an inborn psychological orientation, a naturally greater comfort with the inner world of private experiences. Furthermore, all cultures seem to promote some modesty or diffidence as a way of protecting communal living from the needlessly abrasive assault of self-centered, raw hedonism.[3]

The pathological shyness of those who have suffered disruption in the early development of an acceptable self-image is another matter. As a grown-up, such a person lives under the painful yoke of bashfulness and timidity. Some cover this with mock boldness. Beneath the surface is a chronic fear of other people.

The excessively shy person is usually very self-conscious in negative, self-demeaning ways. The self-image is one of being "unwanted, unloved, ugly, different, uninteresting, lonely or neurotic."[4] Consciously fearing rejection, shy people will do almost anything to avoid risking it. As a result, they are usually silent, hypersensitively monitoring every word and gesture. This is especially true in the presence of strangers, members of the opposite sex, or others who may judge. When they do try to express themselves, they are likely to be hesitant, needlessly soft-spoken, ingratiating, and apologetic. Whenever possible, they simply will try to avoid contact with other people.

This self-protective overreaction does *not* accompany normal shyness. Shy people who have a well-developed sense of self understand that it is the external situation that contributes to embarrassment, rather than some defect in their own character. Unlike the shy self-damaged personality, they come to learn that these anxieties are triggered by reactions to particular people and situations. The normally shy individual also understands that other people are probably subject to equivalent vulnerability.

Pathological shyness constitutes a significant portion of the

87

burden of needless suffering borne by the men and women who seek my help in psychotherapy. Initially most patients complain of fear of rejection as a central source of apprehension and pain. Such a person is astonished to discover that the true underlying problem turns out to be quite the opposite.

Such people cannot get anywhere in overcoming excessive shyness without first discovering that what is truly most frightening is *not* rejection but acceptance, *not* failure but success. The patient begins to go after what he or she wants out of life. When such action results in being accepted and well treated by other people, the pathologically shy individual becomes very uncomfortable. Because these people feel undeserving of such unfamiliar achievement and acceptance, unwittingly they have learned to discredit these pleasurable experiences. A poignant early expression of this self-defeating attitude occurs during the first phase of psychotherapy. The shy borderland patient (in this case a man) cannot believe that I or anyone else could accept him as he is. Encouraging him to hold on to the comforting protection of his distrust for as long as he needs it, I promise to try not to treat him any more acceptingly than he can bear.

Anything that makes him feel worthwhile calls forth the echo of his mother's voice, demanding that he question his presumption. It is as though he can almost hear her demanding, "Just who do you think you are?" Believing even for a moment that he is a satisfactory human being evokes the underlying shameful feeling that he has presumed too much.

It was my parents who started me off down my own painful path of shame and false pride. They are no longer responsible for this trip that I sometimes continue to make. Now the enemy is within. It is only my own overblown ego that shames me. It is only I, still sometimes arrogantly insisting on having higher standards for myself than I would impose on others. How much easier to accept the flaws in others than in myself. To the extent that I cling to being special in this way, I remain stuck with the tediously painful life of the perfectionistic striver. I must get everything right, all the time, or suffer shame. It is far too high

88

a price to pay for maintaining the illusion that I might be able to rise above human frailty.

At such times, I trade off acceptance of myself as an ordinary human being for the idealized image of the special person I might yet become. I give up being satisfied with myself as a pretty decent, usually competent sort of guy who, like everyone else, can feel overwhelmed, make mistakes, and sometimes play the fool. Instead I insist that if only I tried harder, really cared, truly wanted to, I could become that wonderful person who could make my long-dead parents happy. Then they would approve of me. I would be the best. *Everyone* would love me.

My problem remained one of still trying to define who I am and what I'm worth in terms of how other people see me. Embarrassment and (to a lesser extent) shame require an audience of expectant others (whether present or fantasized). In this aspect these discomforts must be understood as primarily *social* experiences, rather than as solely personal or intrapsychic phenomena. Guilt is more self-contained. Embarrassment and shame arise when our foibles are exposed before the eyes of others. While the attention of even a passing stranger in a public situation may be all that is needed for a flawed gesture to be embarrassing, shame requires that they be *significant* others.

When someone clearly is not living up to social expectations, others may feel embarrassed for him or her (as in the case of an audience watching an onstage performer who forgets lines). At such times those who are watching someone else get rattled may undertake the remedial work of restoring the victim's composure, "others may be forced to stop and turn their attention to the impediment . . . their energies are directed to the task of re-establishing the flustered individual, of studiously ignoring him, or of withdrawing from his presence."[5]

It is contagiously discomforting to witness someone else's embarrassment or shame. We are usually tempted to try to do something about it or to act as though it did not happen. Guilt is a more private experience and evokes far less empathy from others.

89

In distinguishing between embarrassment and shame, and again between shame and guilt, I do not mean to imply that these are in any way mutually exclusive categories of experience. It is certainly possible, for example, to feel both guilty and ashamed at the same time.

The complexities of the interactions among such distressing phenomena are many. I may feel guilty over the realization that I am ashamed of something one of my children has done. Or I may find myself embarrassed to discover that I still feel guilty about some of my own youthful indiscretions.

Beyond these basic interplays, I may even have a secret sense of pride that I am such a "good" person that I feel guilty about deeds that others would find acceptable. As a consequence of my pleasure over such a petty moral victory, I may experience a flood of shame at having been pleased with myself for being so virtuous.

The tricks of the imagination are beyond counting. That's part of why it's so difficult to live a sensible life. Human decency seems a fragile commodity, requiring a delicate balance of the pressures to which we subject ourselves and that others impose on us. In the absence of optimal conditions, decency often collapses.

Of necessity, we each mess up again and again as we try to make our way. Still, it behooves us to do our best. We must make our inevitable mistakes, face our foolishness, forgive ourselves as best we can, and go on.

In allowing for penance, atonement, and expiation of misdeeds, guilt is easier to manage than shame. If I do a bad deed, I may feel guilty about that piece of behavior. I have the possibility of being a worthwhile person who has done a bad thing. I can make up for it and I can be forgiven. If, instead, my shortcomings as a human being make it impossible for me to live up to the expectations of significant others, then it is my whole self of which I must be ashamed.

Shame is an overwhelming experience. The root meaning of the word *shame* connotes being wounded in a way so enveloping

90

that it generates a need to cover up. *Guilt* connotes a debt, a specific obligation that can be fulfilled and altered. How much more total is the experience of feeling ashamed, having been caught with my pants down, wishing that the ground would open up so that I could sink into oblivion! Being guilty feels awful, but not so awful as when I feel that I could die of shame.

There is a vast difference between feeling *guilty* about *what I do* and feeling *ashamed* of *who I am*. I can change what I do, but how am I to change who I am?

I may experience guilt when I *choose* to do something that is not permitted—when I lie or steal or cheat. Shame is thrust upon me *involuntarily*. Guilt comes with a particular act. Shame is a total condition. I "find" myself ashamed. It suffuses my whole being.

Ashamed, my insufficient self is exposed to disapproving eyes. There is no particular deed that can be retracted, atoned for, and forgiven. It is easier to face the guilt for doing wrong than the shame for being inadequate.

Shame and guilt arise from different kinds of faulty parenting. Bad mothering makes the child feel shame. The residual sense of being an unacceptable adult gives an anguished voice to the infant's originally wordless response to impersonal treatment. Guilt arises later out of too harsh experiences of moral injunctions traditionally associated with bad fathering. In practice, either parent may elicit one or the other pained response.[6]

Excessive authoritarian fathering creates neurotically guilty anticipation of punishment for transgression against the lawful order of things. Overly demanding mothering breeds shame in borderland personalities. The shamed child comes to fear contempt and eventual abandonment merely because its own separate identity does not completely merge with the self-absorbed mother's all-encompassingly insatiable demand for the closeness of total union.

In an attempt to turn me into the right sort of person, one who would fit as part of their own perfect goodness, my own parents shamed me often and cruelly. "Be nice!" they would

91

say. "Why can't you ever be nice? If you don't have something nice to say, bite your tongue. Better to say nothing at all."

I am sure that my stored-up resentment came through. Eventually they were correct in perceiving that even if my words were nice, my tone was nasty.

Finally, in desperation, I gave up trying to be good. If the only thing I could do well was to be bad, then I would give myself over to being outrageous.

I could tolerate just so much shaming. Paradoxically, too much shaming often produces borderland defiance rather than neurotic propriety. No longer able to bear the overwhelming burden of shame, a child may develop a secret determination to misbehave. The helplessly vulnerable natural face becomes hidden behind a protective mask of spiteful shamelessness.

NOTES, CHAPTER 7

1. Helen Merrill Lynd, *On Shame and the Search for Identity* (New York: Harcourt, 1958), p. 46.

2. Erving Goffman, "Embarrassment and Social Organization," in *Interactional Ritual: Essays on Face-to-Face Behavior* (Garden City, N.Y.: Doubleday, 1967), p. 102.

3. I suspect that this is an evolutionary development by which individuals have come to compromise some portion of their inherent egocentricity in the interest of species survival.

4. Philip G. Zimbardo, Paul A. Pilkonis, and Robert M. Norwood, "A Shrinking Violet Overreacts: The Social Disease Called Shyness," *Psychology Today*, no. 8, May 1975, p. 72.

5. Goffman, op. cit., p. 101.

6. This depends on the particular parent's role and attitude, rather than on gender alone.

CHAPTER 8

Self-Portrait

The vertical division of personality is most often a split between an insensitively detached public image and an excruciatingly vulnerable private vision. No one has demonstrated this division more dramatically than Oscar Wilde. He displayed the narcissistic borderland personality both in his writings and in his painfully flamboyant personal life.

With characteristic seeming shamelessness, he struck outrageously cynical public postures, declaring, "Truth is entirely and absolutely a matter of style."[1] Insisting that Life should be made to imitate Art, he promoted the narcissistic New Individualism of decadent self-indulgence. But nowhere more clearly than in his only novel, *The Picture of Dorian Gray*,[2] did he reveal his secret nostalgia for lost innocence and spoiled purity.

The decadence espoused by Wilde turns out to be a pathetically insistent denial meant to protect him from being overwhelmed by the anguish of his underlying disillusionment. When one of his characters declares that self-development is life's sole aim, he is saying that only by acting in harmony with one's innermost self can anyone find meaning in life. His brazen cult of immoralism turns out to be no more than a desperate way

[93]

of trying to find out who he is. Lacking a cohesive central sense of self, he is forced to create a contrived identity. He must make himself up as he goes along.

Half the hero of Wilde's novel is a physically beautiful androgenous dandy named Dorian. Fully committed to the passionate indifference of self-absorption, he cares nothing for anyone else. All he wants is to lose himself forever in his addiction to the immediacy of his own polymorphous perverse sensuality.

If this decadent young man is one half of the hero, his portrait is the other. Like Narcissus, Dorian falls in love with his own reflected unspoiled innocence.

The sense of his own beauty came on him like a revelation . . . the shadow of his own loveliness, the full reality of the description flashed across him. Yes, there would be a day when his face would be wrinkled and wizened, his eyes dim and colorless, the grace of his figure broken and deformed. The scarlet would pass away from his lips, and the gold steal from his hair. The life that was to make his soul would mar his body. He would become dreadful, hideous, and uncouth . . . but this picture will remain always young. He will never be older than this day of June . . . 'if it were only the other way! If it were I who was to be always young and the picture that was to grow old! For that—for that—I would give everything! Yes, there is nothing in the whole world I would not give! *I would give my soul for that!*[3]

And so he does. All through a life of ever-deepening degradation, Dorian retains his unblemished look of youthful innocence. Without remorse, he exploits, betrays, and destroys other people. Only in the portrait of his soul is the mask of his shame reflected. It serves not so much as a conscience to his dissolute life as an emblem of it. In the portrait, "hideous lines seared the wrinkling forehead, . . . crawled around the heavy sensual mouth . . . coarse bloated hands . . . the misshapen body and the failing limbs."[4]

In the end, by the time he tries to change his ways, even his acts of kindness have become cunning and hypocritical. His inability to maintain a unified self has resulted in an empty, soulless life. Divided, he is his own enemy. By now, *he has become the portrait* of his ageless glamour while his vulnerable human aspect is maintained only in the painting. Dorian decides that he must take a knife to the canvas and destroy this talisman of his secret identity.

All during his clandestinely monstrous life, he has kept the painting hidden away. It is in this locked room that his servants discover him:

When they entered they found, hanging upon the wall, a splendid portrait of their master as they had last seen him, in all the wonder of his exquisite youth and beauty. Lying on the floor was a dead man, in evening dress, with a knife in his heart. He was withered, wrinkled, and loathsome of visage.[5]

Just as it was too late for Dorian to alter his empty caricature of a life, it is sometimes past time when the borderland characters who enter psychotherapy can hope to reclaim an authentic self. Some come too late. Some are unable to stay long enough to restore their lost humanity. Already in his late fifties by the time he came to see me, Archie still vividly remembered having been raised in an orphanage. It was in that impersonal "home," a lifetime ago, that he consciously contrived his stylized pseudoself.

Now a successful "self-made" businessman, he entered therapy complaining that his homemade self was wearing thin. For most of his life, he had portrayed himself to others as "misanthrope and a curmudgeon." For thirty years now he had been "married to an angel." Only his wife understood that all his uncaring bluster was just a front.

But now, in what he described as "the flower of her menopause," his angel was threatening to leave him. She'd had enough of understandingly having to see through his obnoxious behavior. Without her he would have no one. He had made no close friends. He had alienated all of his grown children. No one at work ever appreciated that "inside" he was soft and that he hurt.

Perversely, he had to back off from any sympathetic appreciation of his feelings that I might offer. Kidding and cutting, he would quickly mock both my compassion and his own anguish. He acknowledged that he could not ever remember being able to deal in any other way with his helplessly vulnerable response to tenderness. The only exception was "screwing." Concealed within his "quite a stud" braggadocio, it turned out that only while making love could he allow his unacknowledged needs for baby softness to be met.

Wearily shaking his head, Archie terminated therapy after just a few meetings. He left still boasting that single-handedly he had invented himself. He left admitting that in the end it all had come down to little more than loneliness and high blood pressure. Doing what he could to leave me laughing, he left punchlining our meeting as my trying to "put new wine in old skins."

Until fairly recently, even when such patients came earlier and stayed longer than Archie had, they were usually considered "unsuitable" for psychotherapy. Men and women whose character was developed as protection against early impersonal parenting were judged hopelessly incapable of ever forming the necessary transference relationship with the therapist.

Part of the therapist's problem was an honest clinical misconception. We simply did not yet understand how to help such people. But in large measure, we condemned them because they made it so difficult for us to live out our own idealized self-image.

These borderland characters seemed to feel so special and self-important that often they regarded us with indifference and our therapeutic efforts with contempt. Preoccupied with dreams of boundless glory and adoration, outrageously demanding of attention, they found our offering unsatisfactory.

In those instances when the therapist was valued, treatment soon turned into a nightmare of fending off the devouring demands of the bottomless pit of the patient's seemingly insatiable hunger. Whenever the therapist was included within the circle of narcissistic specialness, it meant that he or she was expected to be the perfect mother so that the patient might feel like the adored infant. Each time the "special" therapist was at all out of touch with baby's needs, the patient would react with rage to the humiliation imposed by mother's insulting lack of empathy. Hurt and angry, the bewildered therapist would soon feel overwhelmingly burdened by the awesome responsibility of attending this tyrannically touchy infantile character who was so impossible to help.

Those therapists who had suffered some early impersonal parenting of their own were especially vulnerable to the onslaught of the patient's discrediting indifference, insatiable hunger, and annihilatingly explosive rage. Unable to tolerate our helplessness before this shattering assault on the hard-won image of ourselves as good people and helpful therapists, we projected blame onto the patients. Moralizing psychiatrically, we accused them of being emotionally shallow, willfully manipulative and totally incapable of love. Diagnostically, we judged them untreatable infantile character disorders. All this was just a way of defending our own narcissistically idealized self-image. Only by condemning them as the all-bad patients could we maintain the grandiose self-portraits of ourselves as the all-good therapists. Again and again, our judgments were clinically confirmed. Like us, these patients were excruciatingly sensitive to ridicule. The worse we made them feel, the more obnoxiously self-important they behaved.

The trouble often began with the very first meeting of the therapist and the narcissistic patient. We had been trained to expect our patients to be garden variety neurotic personalities whose chronically constricted lives had now been brought to crisis by some clearly disabling symptom. How were we to understand the borderland patient who showed up in the consulting room with no clear complaint of curable compulsion, obsession, conversion, or phobia? These characters reported only vague feelings of emptiness and deadness. Often they lived creative lives in which they functioned well but could find no meaning.

Some complained that at times of stress, they felt as though they were about to fall apart. But most often, no matter how great their subjective distress, again and again to their horror, they discovered that they continued to be able to cope. In their earliest years they had too little personal parenting to develop a substantial natural core of individual identity. At a later age, many of these people found ways to invent facades that serve as compensatory hollow self-structures. It is these contrived portraits that allow them to function overtly well while feeling privately vulnerable and brittle. They experience their fragile selves as easily depleted and sometimes threatened with fragmentation.

Often borderland characters live impressively productive lives, successfully convincing others that they are substantially intact human beings. Secretly these people feel like frauds. Living a made-up life, not knowing who they really are, often they cannot tell what is real and what isn't. However colorful they appear to others, subjectively they lack vitality and enthusiasm. They enter therapy without believing this experience will make any real difference in their empty lives. Often they have sought treatment mainly because of some vague understanding that "it is what people do" under such circumstances. They approach the treatment not knowing what to expect, ready to resolve their uncertainty by finding evidence that the therapist is not to be trusted.

Before therapists began to understand the narcissistic shell of distrust and contempt, they counterattacked with covert criticism embedded in clinical interpretations. They told the patients that this protective shell was made up of distorted and displaced reactions defensively mobilized as resistance against the treatment. The patient would then (correctly) understand that he or she was being instructed that these feelings toward the therapist were unwarranted, inappropriate, sick, or bad.

This sort of personal redefinition of the patient by the therapist had often worked in building a treatment relationship with the more familiar neurotic personalities who dependently sought not only our help but our approval. Neurotic patients had in fact transferred onto us old images of harshly restrictive parents who had taught them to constrain even their thoughts of misbehaving. Our covertly critical interpretations recreated fantasies of those original relationships. Fearful now that we might somehow punish them, these neurotics guiltily tried even harder to be good cooperative patients.

Comparable interpretations of the borderland patients' attitudes resulted instead in exaggeration of their initial distrust, and in still more coldly arrogant posturing. Often the end result was the therapist's self-righteously dismissing the patient as both unsuitable and somehow to blame for not having the right sort of attitude toward the treatment. Sometimes it might be the patient who would fire this inadequate therapist. In that case the patient could leave with an outward air of hauteur beneath which there was always a deep private sense of again feeling shamefully unfit for the world of human beings.

More recently, increased understanding of the psychology of the self has become available.[6] Borderland patients are now more likely to be offered the appropriate personal attention they need. More and more often, the treatment flourishes, the patient is transformed, and the therapist's own revised self-portrait is left less flattering.

The change in the therapist's traditional approach must begin with the very first meeting. The patient's contempt and distrust are not to be interpreted away, but to be accepted with empathy. As the therapist, I need only begin by listening attentively. Rather than try to understand the symbolic meaning that lies *behind* the patient's words, I listen only to begin to try to appreciate what those words communicate about how the patient is experiencing being here with me right now.

I remember a woman I will call Elly, whose opening remark during our first meeting was a transparently sardonic "Dr. R. [the referring physician] tells me you're a pretty tough cookie!" I waited for her to go on, but she seemed silently dug in, stubbornly awaiting my reply to her challenge.

Softly I answered, "Sounds like you know *he* thinks I'm tough,

99

and maybe *I* think I'm tough, but *you* will have to have a chance to see for yourself."

Sounding more strident and at the same time less sure of herself, Elly went on to say, "You shrinks think you know it all. We're like specimens under a microscope for you to study, germs for you to classify and control before we start an epidemic."

"Even if I do seem to listen, maybe even seem to understand a little bit, that would just make me more dangerous. You've been fooled before."

More hesitantly, she stammered, "You're the first shrink I've challenged who didn't right away have to defend himself." Elly was quiet a while and then, more confidently, "Maybe I just haven't touched your sore spots yet. I used to be in treatment with a Catholic psychiatrist. All I had to do to pull his chain was to talk about my abortions."

"Maybe this experience could be different, but it's much too early to begin to trust. Who knows? When you find out what upsets me, you may be able to yank me around like you did that other therapist."

Her first shy smile appeared. "You really do listen, don't you?"

All that I had to offer at that moment was attentive listening to what she had to say. It was a genuine attempt to begin to understand what she might be feeling. There was no room for my criticizing or even for questioning her experience of our coming together. All I could try to communicate was that I was listening, trying to understand, and that I wished to accept her vision of our encounter simply because it was hers in particular.

With any patient, it would have been too early for interpretations. With someone so vulnerable that she must come on this strong from the outset, it was too early even to begin thinking about such interventions. All of my attention needed to be focused on making personal contact with this woman. If part of me was off somewhere in my head theorizing about her psychopathology and my therapeutic interventions, her distrust and contempt would soon have been confirmed. Badly used as she had been by other impersonal caretakers, Elly was painfully sensitive to the most well-meaning sorts of intrusiveness and the most benign forms of neglect.

Though the familiar neurotic patient at first seems the more dependently compliant of the two, it is the narcissistic borderland patient who turns out to be capable of totally engrossing attachment to the therapist. The neurotic retains a solidly established separate sense of self, restricted only by horizontal division from those repressed impulses that have been forbidden. It is this same division that serves as a covert bastion of protection against the therapist. The neurotic patient's false mask of compliance is meant to disarm the seemingly dangerous adversary. The projected image of the critical, punitive parent who originally forbade awareness and expression of the now repressed impulses has been transferred onto the therapist. The self-structure of the neurotic is reinforced in the ongoing struggle to retain the repressions of the disavowed impulses.

Much of the therapeutic work with neurotics is a slow, tedious ordeal of gradual chipping away at the defenses. Eventually this allows previously disowned feelings to once again become conscious, acceptable, and have greater options for free expression. By interpreting the unconscious meaning of symbolically disguised communications, the therapist helps the neurotic to recover memories of the threatening childhood experiences that first necessitated the original horizontal splitting off of instinctual impulses.

Dealing with the borderland patient is a very different sort of experience for the therapist. The patient's initial attitude will be one of unavailability ranging from unresponsive apathy or chilling aloofness to deep distrust and bitter contempt. Paradoxically, if this bastion is met with feelingful empathy and genuine acceptance, it can be transformed almost immediately into an intense attachment to the therapist who has been experienced as attentive and understanding. Unlike the neurotic who transfers on to the therapist the image of the unsatisfactory parent he or she had, the narcissistic patient transforms the therapist into the idealized parent he or she would like to have had.

Elly and I agreed to meet for psychotherapy sessions three times a week. Very soon, indirectly she began letting me know that I had become important to her. By the time we had been meeting for just a few weeks, she declared openly that coming to see me had become the only significant experience in her otherwise empty life. The obviously genuine intensity of her immersion in our relationship was made all the more curious by the fact that before coming to therapy, Elly had already been making her way in the world.

Neither emotionally paralyzed nor reclusive, she had advanced several grades on a successful administrative career track. She was married to a man whom she described as treating her kindly. Additionally she had several friends whom she liked and respected. During our first meeting, she registered a single complaint about her life. "The only trouble is that none of it makes any sense. It's as though what goes on in my life has nothing to do with me in particular. I've always felt more dead than alive. Sometimes I thought probably everybody felt that way. Other times I knew it was just me who did, but I wasn't even sure that it mattered. I've only gone to shrinks because my husband seemed to think it would be best."

Elly was not given to indulging herself. She showed no overall hysterical flair for dramatizing her experiences. She was apathetic about everything else in her life except our relationship.

The extent of her general detachment from her emotions is demonstrated in the subjective description of her ocasional tearfulness. "I understand that since I'm crying, it must be that I'm sad. But all I really feel is that my eyes are wet, and if it goes on long enough, my nose will get sore."

At first her attachment to me was expressed in sexual terms, but the initially erotic quality of her dreams and fantasies always quickly gave way to childlike wonder and delight. For example, during our second meeting, she reported the following dream: "I dreamed that as I was leaving our first session, one of us didn't want me to go. At the door of your office we hugged and kissed. You put your tongue in my mouth, and I put my tongue in your

102

mouth. It was the wettest kissing you can possibly imagine. Your spit and mine got so mixed together, we couldn't tell which was which. It was wonderful, the very best dream I've ever, ever had."

My interpretation of the dream went something like this. "Being here with me last time was a wonderful experience for you because you felt that I was so in touch with what was going on inside of you that sometimes you couldn't tell where one of us ended and the other began." She was delighted with my interpretation, and expressed relief that unlike previous therapists, I had not emphasized the obvious sexual implications of the dream.

Elly went on to add that she had been even more frightened that I might experience the dream as implying that being close to her would endanger me. I did not understand what she meant, but for the moment I chose not to ask.

In response to my unasked question, she announced: "I was a toxic baby. I almost killed my own mother before I was even born."

This grotesque self-accusation was made without emotion. In a matter-of-fact way, she went on to describe how, all the time she was growing up, her mother had to worry about Elly's "disaster-proneness." They didn't have that sort of trouble with her sister, so clearly the problem was not mother's but her own. It made good sense that her parents would encourage her sister to stay on at home to attend a local college.

When Elly completed high school at 17, mother announced her parents' graduation gift: "How would you like to live in the nation's capital?" It turned out that all of the arrangements had already been made. Halfway across the country, a government job was waiting, and a temporary place to stay as well. Elly would be leaving for Washington in two weeks.

Mother explained that as a state official, father had connections. He was credited with having arranged for his daughter's new career. But Elly knew better. She was fond of her father and understood that he never acted independently of mother's domination.

Later on in therapy she said sadly that she didn't know how she would have made it without him. At least he hadn't constantly criticized and harassed her as mother had. True, he was a withdrawn, impassive sort of a man, but he had always loved nature and the outdoor life. Sometimes he'd taken Elly camping with him. She always looked forward to their times alone together. But daddy hardly spoke, and there had even been times that he had remained unavailable when she was in danger. Still it meant a lot to her to be taken along, even though more than once he had actually lost her in the woods.

Though it was father whom she missed, once exiled to Washington, Elly only kept in touch with mother. She tried her best to deny that they had sent her away because she was too dangerous to keep around. Simulating a personal life as best she could, Elly diverted her attention from the pain of loneliness by keeping therapeutically busy with work and studies. Her considerable intelligence operated effectively within the contrived immersion in what her mother called "constructive activities," allowing her successful movement along a civil-service career track. Free time was largely absorbed by part-time academic studies that never included poetry, her most treasured secret interest. Elly kept busy, but her heart was not in it.

In her mid-twenties she met and married a man whom she experienced as being much like her father. Inarticulate and unaggressive, he seemed available and uncritical. As Elly went on with her self-exploration in therapy, she began to realize that there were ways in which her husband seemed as much like her mother as like her father. So long as she was passive and compliant he was never actively critical. But whenever Elly began to assert herself or to seem adventuresome, her husband stirred her self-doubt by his own whiningly complaining fears that she would "make trouble" for them.

Both at work and at home, Elly was so vulnerable to the lowering of her self-esteem that even implied criticism would bring her to her knees. Anxious to please, it was easy to ignore her own wishes and well-being in favor of appeasing whoever was dissatisfied with her.

It was not until well into the second year of therapy that she was able to reveal and to explore the unacknowledged contempt in which she held her critics. The appeasement she offered controlled their criticism so easily. Secretly superior, her simulated surrender made no dent in her impenetrable wall of inner detachment.

Eventually this same paradox was evident in her relationship with me. My acceptance made her life worthwhile. Any time she experienced me as disapproving of her, she felt painfully humiliated. But the nature of my importance in her life became clear one day when, a few minutes before our session was to begin, Elly encountered me in the lobby of my office building.

During the session, she was dreadfully upset, completely thrown by finding me "out of place." Eventually she was able to make clear that though our times together were the high points of her week, between sessions she thought of me as having been tucked away in a drawer out of which she could take me whenever she needed me. Ironically, until she had developed a parallel attitude of genuine personal concern for me, she could not reveal this narcissistic possessiveness.

Up to that point she displayed and reported boundless compliance with other people's expectations. If someone was unhappy, she often experienced that distress as her fault. She did whatever she imagined was required to make them feel better. If her offerings were not accepted, she would retreat into petulance, feeling hurt and insulted that her "love" had been rejected. Even while apparently dedicated to pleasing others she had a very different hidden agenda. Not until she had begun to give up her secret sense of being "someone very special" could she admit that for years she believed that "if anyone is saying something that bores me, I feel that, without my having to complain, they should recognize that fact and do something else."

For most of her adult life, Elly had rarely complained about anything to anyone. She tried to be whatever anyone seemed to want her to be. Early in therapy, she labeled her wearing of so many masks by diagnosing herself as suffering from "multiple personalities." All but one of her false faces were compliant.

Only as a stranger on a plane or a train did she speak with un-characteristic confidence, bragging about real and imagined accomplishments. Self-assertively she directed the lively conversation, welcoming the attention and admiration of any other stranger who was willing to listen.

Her more usual mock compliance seemed necessary protection against the destructive mother in whose image she fashioned everyone who knew her. For Elly to acquire a genuine identity of her own, she had to learn to recognize these projections as representations of irrational forces *within* herself.

As she came to feel safer with me this transformation began to take place. The more often Elly experienced me as a sufficiently good enough therapist, the more readily she could begin to tolerate the times she felt disappointed with me. For a long while, she had found me beyond reproach. Any misunderstanding between us was attributed to some imagined flaw in herself. No matter what went wrong she would protect my idealized image by blaming herself and feeling ashamed. Bit by bit, she found herself increasingly able to tolerate expression of the secret rage she felt toward me whenever she was disappointed by my imperfect mothering. I did not need to contrive these failings. Elly observed accurately that from time to time I was too self-absorbed to be sufficiently attentive or empathically understanding.

At first she could not allow herself to experience how angry she became when my behavior frustrated her. She could not yet recognize that even when our relationship felt all bad we were still the same two people whom she usually experienced as all good. She was burdened by the terrifying belief that the result of her open reaction to frustration would be that either she or I would be destroyed.

As her recognition grew, Elly became more openly assertive. It was then that she began to express anxiety about relinquishing her false selves. What if underneath she was really crazy? What if hidden beneath her compliance was a monster that would swallow the whole world? What if, in the course of her self-explorations in therapy, she discovered that, like an onion, once all her outer layers were peeled away, there was nothing left?

For a lifetime, the wearing of her many false faces had reassuringly protected Elly's damaged self-esteem. At those times when she had felt merged with the idealized mother I had become for her, she was temporarily free of her chronic anguished concern with who she *really* was. But the humiliation and later the rage she experienced when she suffered the narcissistic insult of my momentary inattentiveness or lack of empathic understanding left her unprotected by her defensively contrived selves. As she gave up her old ways of living without yet having discovered new ways, she often felt lost in wordless despair. I was pained to see her suffer so. Still, as a psychotherapist, I knew that "one of the first signs of beginning understanding is the wish to die [as] this life seems unbearable, another unattainable."[7]

During that period, Elly needed me to be silently unobtrusive but patiently available. It was a time during which she described herself as "a nonentity," a "ghost searching for a machine," an "amoeba," and a "soul in limbo." Self-examination was "like peering into a black hole in deep space." But peering into that black hole Elly found none of the terrible objects of her apprehension. Seeking her center, she encountered neither lunatic nor savage beast nor the dreaded bottomless emptiness. At first she was shocked and bewildered, and only later amused at the absurdity of discovering that out of that black hole in space . . . out of the pit of nonentity . . . came *Walter Cronkite*, "the Rotarian in all of us."

Could it be that what she feared most was learning that she was no different than anyone else?

The lifelong burden of maintaining multiple false selves was ultimately unrewarding. Even so, it was not easy for Elly to relinquish her chronic sense of personal peculiarity. Accepting her true self would necessitate transforming her craziness into creativity, her secret savagery into nondestructive aggressiveness, and her isolated emptiness into a hunger for risking close personal relationships. Acceptance of her ordinary aspect would require that she give up her martyred secret superiority as well.

Elly's evolving self-acceptance began during the years while she was still in therapy. It began while she was working with me, but after a time she came to see that to complete her growth she would have to separate from me.

During our time together, she had left her husband to explore relationships that promised greater freedom to have a life of her own. When she no longer needed the dulling security of a civil-service career track, she simply quit her job. Living on accumulated pension plan funds, she hoped to give herself the chance to try becoming the poet she had secretly longed to be.

Years later I received a letter from Elly. Enclosed were several of her own published poems. In the letter, she described herself as "no longer a multiple personality tied too tightly to a single all-purpose relationship." She went on to say, "I have become more and more a single self with multiple relationships to fill my many needs." When she had enough money accumulated, Elly gave herself completely to the writing of her poetry and the continuing work on her self. Each time the money ran out, she would work for wages for a while, but only long enough to accumulate enough money to live the way she wanted to for the next few months.

Toward the end of the letter she wrote regretfully of having wasted so much of her adult life stuck in a failed marriage and a dull career. Ironically, it had been her way of walling off what she had experienced as a peculiarly strange and dangerously unstable secret self. She had come to accept that her self included *both* the craziness of her idiosyncrasies and the ordinariness of her Walter Cronkite aspect. With her self-esteem no longer constantly in jeopardy, Elly found that she was free to live as she pleased.

NOTES, CHAPTER 8

1. Quoted in Epifanio San Juan, Jr., *The Art of Oscar Wilde* (Princeton, N.J.: Princeton University Press, 1967), p. 7.

2. Oscar Wilde, *The Picture of Dorian Gray*, ed. Harry Shefter, with an introduction by Leonard R. N. Ashley (New York: Washington Square Press, Pocket Books, 1972).

3. Ibid., pp. 25–26. There were no italics in the original.

4. Ibid., p. 127.

5. Ibid., p. 223.

6. This new vision accrues from the work and writing of many therapists. A major share of the credit must be given to Heinz Kohut for boldly pulling together and setting forth this conceptual advance in two seminal works: *The Analysis of the Self* (1971) and *The Restoration of the Self* (1977) (New York: International Universities Press).

7. Franz Kafka, quoted (without reference to source) by Johannes Pfeiffer, "The Metamorphosis," in *Kafka: A Collectional of Critical Essays: Twentieth-Century Views* (Englewood Cliffs, N.J.: Prentice Hall, 1962), p. 58.

PART III
Self-Contradictions

I am large, I contain multitudes.
. . . .

Do I contradict myself?
Very well then I contradict myself.

—Walt Whitman,
"Song of Myself"

CHAPTER 9

Hide and Seek

Every self is divided. Each includes contradictions that can never be settled once and for all. There may be temporary and partial solutions to the struggles within each of us, but no matter how they balance out, the opposing aspects of our personalities remain in an uneasy state of irrevocable tension.

In every self there is inherent opposition between the perennial polarities masculinity and femininity, between reason and imagination, and between the individual needs and a sense of social responsibility. Each of us must somehow manage to come to terms with the paradox of simultaneously possessing both "higher spiritual consciousness" and base biological instincts. Such dilemmas are too troubling to be faced head-on all of the time. Fortunately, self-awareness fluctuates enough for us periodically to escape feeling overwhelmed by our otherwise insufficient capacity for coping with so much internal contradiction.

There are times when we accurately perceive our position as helpless. A clear conception of the self is basic to feeling in charge of a personal life of one's own. Paradoxically, in situations of helplessness awareness of self can add to the burden of feeling inadequate.

Apart from the clutter created both by our honest errors and by our deliberate irresponsibility, we can each bring to our lives some small measure of effective management. But no matter how wisely and how carefully we may try to conduct our lives, each will run its course well beyond our personal control. Each life will be determined largely by disinterested chance factors, and each will be ended by the impersonal inevitability of death.

All of us suffer total responsibility for a life over which we have only partial control. We each lack sufficient freedom to feel fully in charge of our lives. Even so, everyone must find ways to make this ultimately unmanageable existence personally meaningful. Much of life remains beyond control. At times it seems that all of our efforts may make no appreciable difference. Unable to cope successfully with fate's unpredictable excesses, we are left feeling helpless and hopeless. Sometimes there is nothing we can do to rectify the situation. No matter how hard we try, we are unable to live just as we wish.

When things do not go our way, like the neglected or abused child, we may experience our frustration as deserved. Threatened with lowered self-esteem, we may then fall back on heightened self-deception. At such times, our attention shifts to self-justification. As a result, we sometimes lose sight of our original goals. We insist that *whatever* is happening, we ourselves are blameless, or right, or at least well-intentioned. Denying the reality of our situation, we may posture and pretend that all is just the way we want it to be.

The self-deception required to bolster failing self-esteem is a kind of selective inattention that distorts our vision both of ourselves and of the world. While trying to retain a subjectively positive self-image, we may at the same time be trying to hide our "bad side" from others' view. Explaining away our irresponsible actions, we may project blame and ignore any evidence that belies our professedly good intentions. Either deliberately or unknowingly we may cover up in the service of euphemizing what is going on. Or, if caught red-handed, we may wallow in an excessive display of guilt that is less penitent than prideful.

114

Fooling others always consumes energy and limits freedom. The selective inattention required for *self*-deception can be even more costly. Those who have suffered excessively damaging early childhood experiences end up severely disabled by the radical splitting of the personality required for preserving self-esteem. But even relatively undamaged everyday personalities must endure some divisions of the self. These "normal" bastions are more temporary and less comprehensive than their radical neurotic and borderland counterparts. Even so, any division of the self is emotionally costly. At times we have no choice but to erect such self-protective structures. Too often we may wastefully maintain them beyond the time when they are needed.

Exploration of the horizontally split obsessional neurotic personality and of the vertically split narcissistic borderland personality can each teach us something about the less pathological self-divisions of relatively undamaged everyday personalities. Closer to the normal everyday divisions is a third radically pathological type of divided self, the hysterical personality. Like the obsessional neurotic, the hysteric has not suffered critically damaging childhood experiences until *after* the opportunity for developing a core self.

Both are types of neurotic personality but they are not split in quite the same way. If the borderland personality can be described metaphorically as having been split *vertically*, and the obsessional personality split *horizontally*, the hysteric can be conceived as having been split *on the bias*.

In Chapter 5 I described two horizontally divided personalities, both obsessed with self-control. Max and Martha had developed elaborate defenses for keeping out of touch with their repressed impulses. Hysterics, in contrast, do not seem to care what primitive urges might get out of hand, just so long as they can maintain their biased self-image. Max and Martha substituted reason for emotion, sacrificing pleasure for moral certitude and abandoning action for perfectionistic cautions. They seem willing to appear foolish in the eyes of others and to suffer their own chronic self-criticism if only they could be sure that they

115

would not lose control of their baser instincts. No hysteric worthy of the name would put "proper behavior" ahead of a pleasing self-image.

. Nor does a hysteric rely on the obsessional's careful scrutiny for maintaining the biased image. Without ruminating, justifying, or explaining, hysterics simply insist that things must be just the way they want them to be. Any experience that fits the biased outlook is indulgently overvalued. Whatever challenges the fantasy is willfully denied out of hand. Uncommitted to logic, order, or attention to detail, the hysteric is vague and impulsive. Facts and contradictions are ignored. A simplified fairy-tale vision of the pure self is sustained by exaggerating any vague impression that seems to favor the bias.

In place of confirmable facts and examined ideas, the hysteric substitutes diffuse biased impressions that serve to exaggerate feelings ranging from "So wonderful that I simply must have it," to "So awful that I cannot possibly bear it." This impressionistic outlook is maintained by responding in a confused global way that reduces each experience to simplified categories of either "wonderful" or "terrible" (that is, to fitting or not fitting the fantasy-bound image of the self).

Selectively flighty attention ignores details that might otherwise contradict the desired overall impression. If internal contradictions are to be successfully ignored, complexities in the outside world must be set aside. This selectively biased inattention continuously skews the hysteric's view of self and situation until each emotionally exaggerated experience seems bigger than life. Hyperbole so stylizes both the subjective sense of self and all of its outward expression that the hysteric comes to being a caricature of whatever role the bias supports.

Typically, female hysterics strike us as glamour queens or as adorable little girls. Their male counterparts appear to be romantic adventurers or precious prodigies. In any case, each appears to lack the balancing contradictions that make less exaggerated personalities more believable. It is hard to conceive of the hysterical queen having concerns as ordinary as moving her bowels. Nor do we easily imagine the adorable little girl capable of ruthless competitiveness in an executive career track. The hysterical adventurer seems no more subject to terror than the prodigy to confusion.

The rest of us have to experience doubt and contradictions. Much of our time is taken up with mundane maintenance chores. We can fight dirty if we must. More often than we wish, we are uncertain or afraid. In contrast, the hysteric's energies are devoted to eliminating the ordinary ambiguities of human nature, creating in their place a simplistic impression of the specific self. Characteristics and experiences that do not fit the bias are radically split off as totally incongruent with the primary image. Traditionally, this wholesale denial has been thought of as *dissociation* so complete that, like the degenerate Mr. Hyde within the fastidious Dr. Jekyll,[1] the repressed characteristics might live an intact unconscious life of their own. Patients who live out dissociative episodes, even those billed as multiple personalities, are literary metaphors of the hysterical Double reified into psychiatric actualities. In over twenty-five years of clinical practice, I've never encountered such a person (or persons), nor has any colleague I know directly. The accounts of multiple personalities in both the professional and in the popular literature[2] seem to me more theatrical than psychopathological, more an example of show biz than of a psychological syndrome.

The more familiar, garden variety hysteric melodramatically disavows whole experiences and replaces them with wish-fulfilling fantasies. But this does not result in one or more alternate personalities acquiring a life of its own. Instead, impulses that do not fit the idealized bias are expressed in momentary outbursts of florid behavior that can be discounted almost before they are completed. Typically the hysterical display of emotional fireworks lacks real depth of feeling. Such histrionics are expected to be forgotten as soon as attention is diverted back to the more desirable self-image.

Typically, a hysterical personality might deny that anything I do as a therapist could evoke his or her anger, insisting "I'm simply not capable of feelings as crude as anger. It's just that I am very sensitive, so of course many things upset me." One patient of mine was so "upset" when I would not accept her gift of flowers that she smashed them repeatedly against the coffee table. She was so upset that a moment later we both were covered with a shower of dismembered rose petals. All during her blossom smashing, I was grateful that she had not brought me a more solidly substantial gift and that she was taking her rage out on my coffee table instead of on my head. When the outburst was over, she denied completely having been at all angry, insisting instead that she had simply felt "hurt" by my "mean" refusal to accept her love offering.

Traditionally, hysteria has been a gender-bound personality classification. Patriarchically dominated sexist psychiatry readily joined the less specialized forces of political oppression in condemning women for the very behavior that men had encouraged in them. Women were pressured to concern themselves with appearance rather than with issues of substance, to substitute emotional display for intellectual analysis, and to act as though their actions did not count seriously enough to require women facing up to the consequences of their acts. The grown-up woman was encouraged to act as though she were a favored child whose "loving protector is standing by in the wings, allowing not so much for dependency as a copping out of or relief from the 'realities,' that is, the necessities and constraints to which adults in social situations are subject."[3] The price for saving women from seriousness includes allowing men to write off their protests as merely "hysterical."

It is true that all hysterics are selectively inattentive to experiences that contradict their biased self-image. Characteristically they carry on in willfully attention-demanding ways, gratuitously embellishing reality by telling a little more than the truth. But it is *not* true that all hysterics are women. Many male hysterics are stereotypically heterosexual. It is their exaggerated manliness itself that often reveals their hysteria.

One man I treated made much of his mountain climbing, his

118

hunting, and his prowess as a stud. His Hemingwayesque courage and toughness were always on display. The soft underside
of his nature was denied. He could never admit openly to tenderness, passivity, or fear. Paradoxically, it was in his need to be
admired for supermacho display that he most clearly revealed
himself as a covert little boy seeking approval. The only way
he could act out his dissociated passive dependency was by way
of the periodic sexual impotence for which he sought therapy.

Like his seductive female counterparts, he had been used by
his parents as an emblem of their influence and as an object of
their pleasure. Just as the female hysteric had learned the
adorable little princess pose to get the parental attention she
needed, he had mastered playing the brave little soldier to win
father's acceptance and mother's pampering.

Despite the apparent differences in the biased split of their
exaggerated self-images, both male and female hysterics end
up in a poor trade-off. To win the attention of the contrasexual
parent, each must cater to parental fantasies. Both daddy's girl
and mother's little man end up with an exaggerated sense of
being special that requires their maintaining a glamorized self-
image that has been shaped to fit parental biases.

Some hysterics have to evolve a split that is complex enough to
accommodate the contradictory biases of two opposed parents.
Each demands from the child the opposite of what the other
expects. The child must learn to be both bumbling and accomplished, to be submissive and yet defiant, or to be erotic while
remaining virginally innocent. Faced with having to meet mutually exclusive parental expectation, the child's emotional survival
depends on developing the versatility of a repertory theater
utility understudy.

I once treated a young hysteric whom I will call Bunny. Psychologically, she was a woman of many parts. Professionally,
she had turned this flair for improvisation into a promising
career as an actress. Understandably, she came to therapy complaining of periods of exhaustion and moments of confusion
about what was real and what wasn't.

As we reconstructed her earliest history, it became clear to me that if not for "Amma," emotionally she would not have survived the hazards of borderland damage. Bunny was only a baby when she first called her grandmother by this pet name. It remained the old woman's title until she died when her granddaughter was not yet four years old. Since then, Bunny always referred to her as Amma. Now, more than twenty years later, Bunny could not speak the name without experiencing a flood of tearfully tender feelings. There were no clear memories of her grandmother, only a deep sense of having been enjoyed and well cared for by the old woman.

Had it not been for Amma's good-enough surrogate mothering, it is difficult to imagine that, left to the inadequate care offered by her actual parents, Bunny could have developed a cohesive core self.

Once Amma was gone, Bunny had to turn to her biological mother for the care she needed. Even as a small child, Bunny accurately perceived mother's shallow interest in her as only superficially caring attention. Mother had long been too depressed to be fully aware of her children's needs. Behind her unconvincingly displayed smile was chronic dissatisfaction, often denied but never entirely hidden.

Bunny's only hope lay in curing the smiling depression that restricted mother's availability. Early on, she dedicated herself to consoling her disappointed mother. Sacrificing her own wishes, the child dutifully accepted and tirelessly pursued all of the many music and art lessons that mother's aspirations demanded. They soon filled all of her "free time." In order to fulfill mother's own broken dreams, the child too learned to hide her own discontent.

Theoretically, it would have been possible for Bunny to look to father for the good mothering she needed. But for many years father had been a marginal alcoholic. When his own mother (Amma) died, he drank more and more. In the passive reserve of his sobriety, he was neglectful of the children. Whenever he got too drunk to be blamed for what he'd done, he abused and exploited them.

As the oldest daughter, Bunny was not subjected to the unwarranted brutal punishments that father imposed without
warning on the other "troublemaking" children. She was his
"little darling." He would never hurt her because she was so
"cuddly." Instead of being whipped for making trouble, Bunny
danced for her father. As a reward he fondled her. Though
pleased to receive his special attentions, understandably Bunny
was as frightened and as confused as any incestuously used little
girl would be. Just as she was entering puberty, father left the
family. When the stepfather who took his place made sexual
advances toward the then young teenage Bunny, she was even
surer that her own father would not have abandoned the family
if only she had been "more cooperative."

During the two years between husbands, and then again when
the second one deserted her, mother appointed Bunny guardian
and caretaker of the three (and then four) younger children.
The girl was expected to keep up her role as family entertainer
as well, but any seriously self-serving pursuit of her own career
was discouraged. Bunny learned to achieve on demand, to pursue her own interests only in secret, and to value her "gift" of
compassion for the needs of others.

It is no wonder that by the time she sought psychotherapy in
her mid-twenties, Bunny had become an artistically accomplished wan and weary hysteric. Instead of simply phoning my
office to arrange for an initial appointment as other prospective
psychotherapy patients would do, Bunny wrote me a long dramatic letter describing both her promising artistic efforts and
her unhappy love relationships. She wrote to me of her hope
that I would accept her as a patient, as well as of her fear that
our meeting would turn out to be yet another of her disappointing pursuits of "an unavailable father-figure."

So that I would better understand who she was (and value her
enough to accept her as a patient), Bunny had enclosed "a packet
of original poems and drawings." I responded to her promotional
efforts with a short note of my own. In it I let her know that
though I had not opened her "packet," I did take on new patients
from time to time. Like anyone else, she was free to call my

121

office for an appointment. If we could agree upon a mutually acceptable hour, we would meet to see whether or not we liked each other enough to work together.

Breathless with excitement, a few days later she called to make an appointment. The hysterical intensity of her enthusiasm was repeatedly deflected during our first meetings, as again and again she pressed for special concessions that I would not grant. In place of her requested insurance contract compromises, revised appointment scheduling, and delayed payment plans, I offered reflections of her feelings and interpretations of her behavior.

With each disappointment her hysterical fires were quickly rebanked by the wonderful experience of "at last discovering a man who is gentle with me without letting me get away with pushing him around." Bunny was soon caught up in the sudden swirl of sometimes wonderful, sometimes terrible, but always dramatically transforming emotional experiences. All of these extravagant adventures pivoted on her unbelievable good fortune in having found someone as "magic" as me. We had begun meeting late in the spring. I understood that our honeymoon might well end with my approaching month-long summer vacation.

As the time of our separation drew near, Bunny grew increasingly tense. Then without warning one day, she came in ecstatic about how these few weeks of knowing me had changed her entire emotional perspective. A lifetime of psychological problems had been resolved. Her depressing self-doubts, her crippling anxieties, and even her painfully messed-up relationships with men, all had been miraculously healed by my loving acceptance. I reflected her good feelings without challenging this sudden recovery. In exploring her fantasies with her, I did invite Bunny's attention to some subtle indications of unacknowledged dark feelings and masked wish to do something for me. She seemed too excited to pause long enough to examine these details. Too excited to attend to "trivia." She was thoroughly intolerant of any of my contradictions to her mood. For the re-

122

mainder of the session Bunny was absorbed in increasingly extravagant descriptions of how my love had saved her.

The following day she was sullenly silent for the first ten minutes of our next session. When it was clear to her that her castle would not be stormed, she stuck her head out of the tower window so that I could see that she was crying. After a bit she told me that she was hurt and angry: "Yesterday you could see that I was a little girl trapped on a merry-go-round, but you wouldn't rescue me. You just sat in the audience getting off on watching me perform on that moving circular stage. You're the therapist so you must have known that I was hiding my bad feelings about your vacation so that I wouldn't spoil your good time." It was the first of our many explorations of how Bunny denied her negative feelings so that she could be everything she imagined I expected her to be, and of her petulance each time she once more found me "too mean" to take care of her.

For a long while whenever Bunny experienced disappointments such as this, her petulance was followed by a naive display of sexual seductiveness. She went so far as telling me that she was a talented artist not only in the studio, but in the bedroom as well. Her most dramatic posturing as *la femme fatale* usually seemed to be more like a very little girl playing dress-up. One time she described a wishful fantasy that therapy could be conducted with her lying passively on her back at my feet while I made her do whatever was best for her. She was coyly delighted when I acknowledged the erotic aspects of her fantasy, but nonplussed when I reframed it as an image of an infant in a crib awaiting its mother's making sure it was well fed, warm, and dry.

Gradually, Bunny's biased patterning of her self-image and of her behavior with others was clarified by her realization, "*I need to fit perfectly into someone else's mold. Otherwise, I experience all my own feelings.*" The disavowed painfully unacceptable emotions had to be reclaimed as her own. First came fragments of rage toward the people who had exploited her. Each angry explosion needed to be followed by a piece of grief-work

123

as she learned to mourn the childhood she had missed and would never ever have.

She lived a marketplace life of swapping seduction and accomplishment for "love." These trade-offs could never be adequate compensation for Bunny's not having been enjoyed for herself. Her moments of retaliation were not much better. Whatever the spiteful satisfaction of making sure that her lovers did not get their way, it never made her feel securely safe from the helplessness of being loved on consignment. Worse yet, the refusal to mourn kept her trapped in a search for other abusive parent substitutes with whom this time she would work out a happy ending.

Bunny's discovery of all of the unacceptable denied feelings that did not fit her biased self-image took a while. Learning to live with the contradictions took her even longer.

Like other hysterics, Bunny counted on simple seduction to solve problems that require far more complex solutions. Whether male or female, the hysteric is a neurotic personality whose divided self is most often split on a sexist bias. But you don't have to be a hysteric to find yourself needlessly gender-bound. None of us is entirely free of the distortions and the divisions imposed by sexist expectations. It is demanded of us that we be either completely male or completely female. The imposed bias requires that gender be once and for all pure, simple, and without contradiction. A man must be a man, and a woman a woman, each all of one and none of the other.

NOTES, CHAPTER 9

1. Robert Louis Stevenson, *Dr. Jekyll and Mr. Hyde*, with an introduction by Abraham Rothberg (New York: Bantam Books, 1967).

2. Corbett H. Thigpen and Hervey M. Cleckley, *Three Faces of Eve* (New York: Popular Library, 1974); Flora Rheta Schrieber, *Sybil* (New York: Warner Books, 1974).

3. Erving Goffman, *Gender Advertisements* (Cambridge, Mass.: Harvard University Press, 1979), p. 5.

CHAPTER 10

The Better Half

. . . the original human nature was not like the present but different. The sexes were not two as they are now, but originally three in number; there was man, woman, and the union of the two, having a name corresponding to this double nature, which had once a real existence, but is now lost, and the word "Androgynous" is only preserved as a term of reproach.

. . . the primeval man was round, his back and sides forming a circle; and he had four hands and four feet, one head with two faces, looking opposite ways, set on a round neck and precisely alike; also four ears, two privy members, and the remainder to correspond. He could walk upright as men now do, backwards or forwards as he pleased, and he could also roll over and over at a great pace, turning on his four hands and four feet, eight in all, like tumblers going over and over with their legs in the air; this was when he wanted to run fast.

. . . the man was originally the child of the sun, the woman of the earth, and the man-woman of the moon, which is made up of sun like their parents. Terrible was their might and strength, and the thoughts on their hearts were great, and they made an attack upon the gods;

. . . the gods could not suffer their insolence to be unrestrained. At last, after a good deal of reflection, Zeus [decided on] a plan [to humble their pride and improve their manners; [he said:] "men shall continue to exist, but I will cut them in two and then they will be diminished in strength and increased in numbers; this will have the advantage of making them more profitable to us. They shall walk upright on two legs, and if they continue insolent and will not be quiet, I will split them again and they shall hop about on a single leg." He spoke and cut men in two, like a sorb-apple which is halved for pickling, or as you might divide an egg with a hair, and as he cut them one after another, he bade Apollo give the face and the half of the neck a turn in order that the man might contemplate the section of himself: he would thus learn a lesson of humility. Apollo was also bidden to heal their wounds and compose their forms. So he gave a turn to the face and pulled the skin from the sides all over that which in our language is called the belly, like the purses which draw in, and he made one mouth at the centre, which he fastened in a knot (the same which is called the naval); he also moulded the breast and took out most of the wrinkles, much as a shoemaker might smooth leather upon a last; he left a few, however, in the region of the belly and navel, as a memorial of the primeval state.

. . . After the division the two parts of man, each desiring his other half, came together, and throwing their arms about one another, entwined in mutual embraces, longing to grow into one, they were on the point of dying from hunger and self-neglect, because they did not like to do anything apart; and when one of the halves died and the other survived, the survivor sought another mate, man or woman as we call them,—being the sections of entire men or women,—and clung to that.

. . . They were being destroyed, when Zeus in pity of them invented a new plan: he turned the parts of generation round to the front, for this had not been always their position, and they sowed the seed no longer as hitherto like grasshoppers in the ground, but in one an-other; and after the transposition the male generated in the female in order that by the mutual embraces of man and woman they might breed, and the race might continue; or if man came to man they might be satisfied, and rest, and go their ways to the business of life: so ancient is the desire of one another which is implanted in us, reuniting our original nature, making one of two, and healing the state of man. Each of us when separated, having one side only, like a flat fish, is but the indenture of a man, and he is always looking for his other half. . . . And when one of them meets with his other half, the actual half of himself, . . . the pair are lost in an amazement of love and friendship and intimacy, and will not be out of the other's sight, as I may say, even for a moment: these are the people who pass their whole lives together; yet they could not explain what they desire of one another. For the intense yearning which each of them has towards the other does not appear to be the desire of lover's intercourse, but of something else which the soul of either evidently desires and cannot tell, and of which she has only a dark and doubtful presentiment.

. . . Suppose Hephaestus, with his instruments, to come to the pair who are lying side by side and to say to them, "What do you people want of one another?" they would be unable to explain. And suppose further, that when he saw their perplexity he said: "Do you desire to be wholly one; always day and night to be in one another's company? for if this is what you desire, I am ready to melt you into one and let you grow together, so that being two you shall become one, and while you live a common life as if you were a single man, and after your death in the world below still be one departed soul instead of two—I ask whether this is what you lovingly desire, and whether you are satisfied to attain this?"—there is not a man of them who when he heard the proposal would deny or would not acknowledge that this meeting and melting into one another, this becoming one instead of two, was the very expression of his ancient need. And the reason is that human nature was originally one and we were a whole, and the desire and pursuit of the whole is called love.[1]

Plato's tale of *Androgyne* is a light-hearted mythic account of the origins of our experienced incompleteness in the absence of the Other. The original intent focuses on how when separated we pursue the beloved as if he or she made up the missing half of our divided self. Those most driven and possessed by such headlong pursuit fail to recognize that some of the complementary qualities sought in the beloved can be discovered in the contrasexual aspect of each of our individual selves.

Acceptance of our fundamentally androygnous nature does not take the place of heterosexual love. In itself, it makes us neither hermaphroditic nor bisexual. Androgyny is merely one of the many different dualities that comprise a complete self. Unrecognized, it makes relationships between men and women more desperate than they need be. Accepted, it makes members of the opposite sex seem less alien and so lessens the animosity between us.

Some divisions of the personality are largely the result of damaging experiences. One clear example is the vertical split that arises out of impersonal parenting during the first three critical years of early development of a psychological self-structure. Another is the neurotic exaggeration of the horizontal split resulting from later, overly harsh and restrictive parenting. The nature of the beast already leaves identity at times confused and uncertain and makes it necessary to delay, compromise, even to deny some individual instinctual urges in the service of group living and of longer-term goals.

Apart from the developmental effects of certain kinds of damaging parenting, every one of us struggles with certain seemingly inevitable divisions of the self. Even with good-enough mothering, and with just, accepting fathering, we each must support a self that somehow encompasses the inherently contradictory vectors of human nature.

Less-than-optimal early experiences may exaggerate the conflict and ambiguity about exactly who we are and how we are to manage the opposing forces. But even the best of parenting cannot save us from the problems that come of being an animal who is self-aware. Some of the more obvious endless struggles within each of us turn on the ultimately unresolvable issues of sexual identity, morality, sanity, and self-sufficiency. There is no way of once and for all settling exactly the question of just who we are. In what proportions are you male or female, good or bad, rational or irrational? Amid these dilemmas, we cannot even finally decide to what extent we are each really on our own, or irretrievably incomplete without the other.

In the literature of the Double, Virginia Woolf[2] rightly embodies the shadow of her protagonist *within* the self. Much of the perennial struggle of the sexes is clearly an interpersonal

128

matter *between* men and women. But the political issues are hopelessly confused by the internal male/female oppositions *within* each of our personalities. Whatever the needed political actions, improving these will also depend heavily on the transformation of individual selves. Any hope of viable political change requires that each man gain greater acceptance of his feminine aspect and each woman come to terms with her masculine side.

Woolf's satirical biography begins with Orlando as a sixteen-year-old boy growing up in the Elizabethan age. In mock heroic posture, he spends much of his time lunging, plunging, and slicing the air with his blade. The object of his bold attack is the family trophy of an enemy's head, the skull of which hangs suspended by a cord from the attic ceiling. By the end of the book, this same Orlando has become transformed into a thirty-six-year-old contemporary woman poet.

One of the pivots in this delightful transformation into creative androgyny is an evocative shipboard episode. The woman Orlando, masquerading as a man, encounters Shell, a man masquerading as a woman. As they must, they fall in love, each feeling better understood than ever before. At first they hesitate to reveal their "real" identities. Once they do, their happiness is consummate, but he can hardly believe that she is not really a man nor she that he is not really a woman.

Today many people agree that to become a complete person, each man must come to terms with his feminine aspect and each woman with her masculine side. This heightened awareness owes much to the influence of two contemporary cultural political forces, the human potential movement and the women's liberation movement. Before their impact, some people already understood that within each man dwelt the soul of a woman, and within each woman the shadow of a man. Still, without these liberating sanctions, awareness of this second self had not been enough to make this Double acceptable. The contrasexual aspect was usually considered a despicable flaw to be overcome rather than a valued resource to be embraced.

If a man did not somehow rid himself of any sign of femininity, he was accused of personal failure ranging from cowardice to perversion. Like the man accused of being "chicken" or "a fag," a woman who did not contain what was considered her lusty, aggressive masculine aspect would be condemned as a "whore" or as a "castrating bitch."

To some extent, fashions change the image of what is ideally masculine and what is feminine in a particular age, place, or social class. It may not be possible to be sure what (if anything) in all of this is basically biological and what is acquired through social conditioning. However, it is clear that pressured to be out of touch with *whatever* is considered to be their contrasexual underside, both men and women tend to become exaggerated stereotypes of what they are expected to be.

Compensating for imagined flaws in their sexual identities, they develop pseudopersonal caricatures of their respective masculinity and femininity. Out of these compensatory exaggerations come the stereotyped bravado and intellectual rigidity of men, the apparent frailty and emotional liability of women. The more each gender exaggerates its pose, the more desperately dependent and ruthlessly manipulative they become with one another. On their own, Rhett Butler and Scarlett O'Hara are each incomplete. Whatever the cost, they must have one another.

The human potential movement provided sensitivity training and encounter groups in which men were encouraged to acknowledge aspects of themselves that had traditionally been rejected as effeminate. Within these seemingly safe settings for emotional experimentation, a man would be provided with the facilitating exercises and the group support needed for discovering and expressing his newfound tenderness and vulnerability. For the first time in their adult lives, some men could shed their tears openly. Ironically, in this setting any man who had excessive difficulty in showing his feminine aspect might then be accused of not being "man enough" to reveal his soft side.

To some extent, the human potential movement supported female self-assertion, but women found expression of this traditionally male aspect better supported by their own liberation groups. Feminist issues go far beyond simple assertiveness training. Still the movement has provided much support for raising women's consciousness about the intense resentment hidden beneath their stereotyped submissiveness. This hidden "masculine" anger serves a woman better when claimed as politically legitimate motivation for actively changing her situation. Explorations of these transitions have been written about extensively in the feminist literature, and indeed might well be best told entirely from the woman's point of view.

I will focus instead on constraints I have suffered as a male that seem the reciprocal of women's oppressively being robbed of their assertiveness. Not only was I not to "cry like a girl"; additionally, I had to learn to "stand up and fight like a man."

My father boasted that he had not cried at either of his own parents' funerals. Denying that it hurt not to be allowed expression of his emotional vulnerability, he claimed his impassivity as a matter of stoic virtue. Again and again he explained to me that it was simply that he was a man, and, as everyone knows, "Only babes and women cry."

As a child, my behavior, attitudes, and self-evaluations were shaped largely by my parents' needs and values. Yet such teachings were not all simply personal expressions of these particular parents. Like all families, in part they served as an agent of the culture, mediating the influence of the larger group in a partially unwitting process of turning out an individual who would be acceptable to the society in which he or she is to live.

Some of the values that the family encourages are also reinforced by other cultural agents, such as the schools, the communication media, and the child's peer groups. In our culture, for example, shaming plays an important part in discouraging deviation from the differential roles that our sexist society demands of boys and girls. Boys are made to feel inadequate if they are not tough, competitive, and "rational." Girls are made to feel flawed if they are not compliant, nurturing, and emotional. Boys are expected to become tough-minded breadwinners,

131

girls to be tenderhearted wives/mothers. A male need only "be a man!" but a female must be a "*good* woman." There is much about sexual role expectations in our culture that involves an arbitrary and deadly stereotyped differentiation.

In this context, it is enough to say that the differences currently exist and that shaming maintains them. The frequency with which, as a kid, I fought with other boys, is a measure of just how effective this cultural shaming can be. A boy often ends up less afraid of risking the killing or maiming of himself or another than of taking the chance that he might be seen by others as a coward or a sissy. In my own Jewish-American family, my mother was the dominant figure and my father the appeasingly submissive supplicant. Despite this subcultural variation from the dominant culture, I, too, was raised under the sloganized constraint of "A man must be ready to fight for what he wants. Don't ever be a sissy."

My earliest recollection of this aspect of being a boy/man was my father's buying me two pairs of boxing gloves for my fifth birthday. Despite my reluctance, he immediately insisted that I put on the gloves with him so that he could teach me how to defend myself. My mother stood by making anxious noises about her baby's getting hurt. In a rare show of assertion in that relationship, my father waved her off as though women have no conception of the meaning and consequences of violence. We put on the gloves and he knelt facing me (just as if that made us equals).

By encouragement and instruction he got me past my uncertainty and into swinging wildly at him. He was careful not to hurt me. Unfortunately, he was not so careful about protecting himself. Within minutes I had struck him squarely in the nose. The blood poured out of his nostrils and down across his lips. I was overwhelmed by the frightening consequences of my power. My father tried to reassure me that he was all right but my mother became visibly upset.

Suddenly she was shouting at my father: "What did I tell you? How foolish to get boxing gloves for such a wild boy. He

132

doesn't care about anyone else. See how he hurts his father. Next he'll hurt me and everybody else around."

In fairness, I believe that my mother did not really want me to fight. She believed that fighting was bad, something only Gentiles did. Yet there were times when she sent me out on errands that took me out of our Jewish lower-middle-class enclave, knowing full well that I was likely to be stopped by some assaultive group of teenagers from the neighboring parish who would accuse me of being a "Christ killer." At such times my mother's explicit instructions were: "Don't fight, but *never*, *never* deny that you are a Jew." She seemed to want me to be well behaved, but did little to help me to avoid occasions of sin.

I fought a lot as a kid, not wisely and not well, but certainly often. Not thinking that I was worth much, I did not expect other children to like me. I sought attention on the streets as I had learned to get it at home—by making trouble. Even as a little kid, I didn't know how to make friends or how to join a group of other children at play. My style of social entry was to take their ball, to tease them, or to jump on some other kid's back. This usually resulted in my getting beaten up and then eventually being accepted, though as something of a scapegoat.

When I did fight as a kid, it was from a peculiar position. I was too scared *not* to fight lest I be humiliated as a coward, and yet I was too scared to *really* fight lest I do something unacceptably brutal. As a result, I began most fights, performing very poorly. It wasn't until I had been hurt enough to begin crying that I would finally fight back with some fury.

A peculiarly dramatic instance of this was my prolonged war with Charlie Hood. Charlie was one of the few non-Jewish kids in the neighborhood. The son of one of the local building superintendents, he was a tough kid whose warrior pose covered his own shame of feeling like a misfit.

For a while when I was eleven or twelve, Charlie Hood beat me up three or four times a week, and always in front of everybody. All of the kids who hung out in the neighborhood would stand around and watch. I don't know how I volunteered for the position of victim, but somehow together Charlie and I worked out that contract.

He never beat me up too badly but always enough to make me feel just awful. He was a good street fighter, restricting his brutality just a bit so that he could remain acceptable to the rest of those middle-class kids. I, on the other hand, was very uneven as a fighter. For one thing, I had never hit him in the face. (My mother had told me that that was not the thing to do.)

One afternoon after school Charlie started beating on me in front of a girl on whom I had a crush. For the first time in my unhappy relationship with Charlie Hood, I overcame my own fear of being seen as a shamefully brutal, lower-class street fighter. Being humiliated in the eyes of this girl was even more shameful. And so in the midst of the fight I punched Charlie right in the mouth. He couldn't believe it. I could hardly believe it myself.

Charlie stopped the play at once. He took me down to the park and we both washed our faces at the fountain. Charlie announced to everyone that I was a tough guy, that he admired me, and that we would be friends from then on. That ended months of regularly scheduled defeat.

Over the years I have often been stuck with this macho pride, this fear of losing my honor. But in truth I have lost my honor in that sense many times. Even as a grown man, in telling my stories of the past I felt compelled to bill myself as a great street fighter. Only now can I confess that I was really more of a chronic street casualty.

As a young kid I fought and fought. It made no sense, but I was uncertain, felt incompetent, and just didn't know how to get along any other way. There were many times when I didn't want to fight, but I was too ashamed to risk being called a coward or a sissy. Better to end up a bloody mess or hurt someone else much worse than I would have wished than to be considered a chicken or a fag.

As an early teenager I did eventually graduate to becoming a marginal member of a fighting street gang. I pretended that

134

I was a better and more enthusiastic fighter than I ever really was. There was some danger and I did fight sometimes, but mostly I hung around the edges of the gang, reaping unearned glory.

"All he knows how to do is fight and to get into trouble, that awful boy. If only he really loved us, if only he really cared about the future, if only he really, really tried, he could be a good boy (like all the other nice Jewish boys in the neighborhood). But no, that's too hard for him. He can't even get along with other children. All he knows how to do is to fight and to get into trouble."

This is how my mother spoke *of* me. This is how my mother spoke *to* me. This is how I came to (mis)behave. This is one of the ways I came to be ashamed of myself. My father often helped by implying that if I were only tougher and a better fighter, I could avoid most battles and win the rest. I was shamed by my father and by the culture if I did not fight, shamed by my mother if I did.

My last teenage fight took place in the local poolroom when I was about seventeen. I had been playing Chicago with a fellow about a year older than I, each of us trying to hustle the other. He had a friend with him whom I didn't know and who was making wisecracks to distract me from my game. Leaning over the table, I went on stroking. Without looking up, I responded to one of those sotto voce asides by asking the fellow with whom I was playing, "Who is this schmuck you brought along?"

The friend must have walked up to me quietly as I continued to stroke. Without warning he punched me squarely in the jaw. I was knocked against the wall. Quickly enough, I recovered from the blow and rushed at him. We began to exchange the pulls and poundings of that peculiar street-fighting combination of wrestling and boxing I had found myself caught up in so many times before.

Halfway through the fight, with neither of us clearly moving toward victory, we were deadlocked across the billiard table. It had gotten noisy and a crowd had gathered. Suddenly Nunzio

135

was upon us. He was a powerful young man whose father owned the poolroom. "All right, break it up and take it outside," he said (probably for the fifteenth time that week). "No fighting in here. This is a poolroom."

Now it was time to take it outside and finish it off. Suddenly I knew it didn't make any fucking sense.

My opponent said, "Let's go."

In a quieter voice, I answered, "No, not me, I'm not going. You can be the winner. I'm finished with fighting."

There was much taunting and name-calling from the guys who had gathered around us, and a look of devastating contempt from my opponent. I could feel that shame of "chickening out." For the first time, it came embedded in the relief of knowing that never again would I have to fight if I didn't really want to.

I didn't fight again until I was about twenty-three. On the basis of student deferments I had delayed induction into the army for as long as I could. I was finally drafted shortly before the end of the Korean conflict. My sons were as yet unborn, and therefore I had not yet been instructed as to my right *not* to participate in a political war I had not chosen.

During basic training, we draftees were stripped of our civilian identities. Our clothing was taken and our hair cut short. Our personalities and names replaced by uniforms and numbers, we were kept under a barrage of exhausting physical demands and demeaning authoritarian criticism. It was the only way to turn a random group of peaceful citizens into a platoon of professional murderers in a few short weeks. Successfully robbed of my usual constraints, I was soon sufficiently edgy to feel ready to kill. Unfortunately, in the dumb way the army sets this up, the only people there to assault were my comrades in arms.

There were two incidents. In one, a tough little man from Boston marched behind me, always managing to step on my heels. It took a couple of weeks before I realized that it was not stupidity but spite that led him to treat me this way. I asked him not to do it. I told him not to do it. I begged him not to do it. Nothing worked.

Then one day as we broke ranks he came into the barracks just behind me. Even as we were going up the steps he stepped on my heels. That tore it! I turned around and threw him down the few steps he had climbed. Fortunately, we were not at the head of the stairs or I probably would have killed him in the process. He was not hurt, but he had been humiliated in front of his friends. To ward off his own shame, impulsively he pulled his bayonet as if to stab me.

I didn't stop to think for a moment before going into a Bogart posture. In a way that effectively stopped the action, I commanded, "Put away that pigsticker or I'll make you eat it." Fortunately, he overcame his shame and backed down, laughing it off—otherwise one of us would have gotten killed.

Several days later in the basic training program, a second incident occurred. I had been married just four months at the time. The forced separation was very painful. Now I learned that wives of trainees could visit the camp on weekends. There was even a guest house at which the couples could stay together.

I went to our corporal and asked him how this could be arranged. He told me he would check with the first sergeant and let me know. In the barracks the following night I asked him what he had found out. He was obviously uneasy about his earlier display of consideration. In retrospect I believe he was made even more uneasy by having to give me disappointing news.

Embarrassed by the pressure of the watching audience of recruits gathered around us, he got tough with me: "The first sergeant says that nobody gets to use the guest house until after the fourth week of training. I guess you'll just have to wait till then to fuck your wife." Almost automatically, I grabbed him by the shirt front and put him up against the barracks wall. The other recruits grabbed my arm. The corporal muttered an apology. If not for that I think I would have beaten his brains out.

137

I believed I was defending my wife's honor. Really I was defending my own macho image. Assaulting this man could only have made it harder for me to arrange to be with my wife. It could easily have resulted in my being court-martialed and imprisoned in a military stockade. It simply did not matter. All that mattered was my humiliation.

I did not fight again for several years. The next incident took place in Greenwich Village. After I got out of the army my wife and I moved to New York. By then we had two young children. One night I was out with a friend, a man with whom I had gone to graduate school, a psychoanalyst.

As we walked down Tenth Street that evening toward my apartment building, we spotted a group of seven or eight older teenagers approaching us. My friend was not streetwise. He simply went on talking of Michelangelo. Immediately alerted by my paranoia, I grew silent.

The first of these teenagers came pushing between us. Out of courtesy, my friend backed off. I knew that if a couple of these guys pushed through we'd be surrounded and that would be it. Grabbing the first kid by the shoulders, I spun him back into his group.

The gang of teenagers began a singsong of nasty taunting. It became clear that they were underprivileged kids from Chelsea, the impoverished neighborhood that abuts what they saw as the opulent and self-indulgent Village. What's more, they were in a transitional rite bridging that difficult void between boyhood and manhood. In order to disown the shameful softness in themselves, they sought out Village homosexuals to beat up. Their taunts implied that they believed that my friend and I were gay lovers. To show that they were not, they were about to do us in.

Seeing that we were close to my building, and having better sense and less shame than I, my friend ran for the apartment house. I stood and fought. Absolutely furious at being violated, I began swinging wildly, pummeling any kid I could get my hands on. Fortunately, they were so uncertain about their own status that they backed off before my fury. Were they more sure of themselves, they could have killed me. Were I more sure of my own worth, like my friend, I would have run away.

Not until they left did I turn and walk to the house. My friend stood in the hallway. Again and again he apologized. He had done the only thing that made sense in the situation. Now he was ashamed! We went upstairs and told my wife the story. It was only then that I discovered that I was bleeding profusely. I had been hit on the head with some kind of weapon.

As my wife tried to nurse the wound, my fury continued. With blood running down my back, I paced the floor muttering angrily about what I would do to those dirty motherfuckers if I ever laid my hands on them again. The impact of early shaming was still in operation. Instead of terror and then relief, I had felt only anger and frustration.

While we were living in the Village, I commuted to work at Trenton State Hospital. The travel time became a burden and so eventually we moved out to New Jersey. We wanted to live on a farm and eventually were able to do this for several lovely years. During the interim, we lived briefly in an inexpensive crackerbox housing development on the outskirts of the city. Our neighbors were mainly blue-collar families. They resented our being better educated, as we resented their being better paid.

The social contrast was made symbolically clear on Sunday mornings. All week I had to wear a business suit, shirt, and tie. On Sunday mornings and during all of my time off, I wore my Village costume, an old pair of blue jeans, work shoes, and a faded denim workshirt. The bricklayer next door emerged each Sunday in plaid sport jacket, neatly pressed slacks, fine silk tie, and handmade Italian shoes.

I did not mind the social distance so much as I did the open antagonism. That July Fourth weekend our neighbors were having a long, loud cookout in their backyard. One of our kids was sick and we could not sleep. Their off-key singing and boisterous fooling around went on into the early morning hours.

Finally I got up and went next door. I told them they were keeping us awake and asked them to quiet down.

In response came the drunken challenge: "If you don't like it, stand up and fight like a man!" It made no sense to me to fight about this. I turned and sadly shuffled back to the house. The cookout crowd jeered.

Shamefacedly, I explained the situation to my wife. She was lovely about it. She assured me that for her, my being a man and taking care of my responsibilities to our family in no way involved having to get into a fistfight with a noisy, drunken neighbor. She let me know that the things she valued in me as a man included my being able to free myself of the willfully destructive pride that might have driven me to do battle in such a situation. I cried. She held me. It was good.

There were no more such confrontations for a long, long time. Living on the farm was a wonderful experience of finding out how much we had to offer each other when there was enough physical and psychological space around us so that we might really get to know each other in new ways. After several years, in the interests of the children for whom the isolation began to become restrictive, and in the service of my finding a more satisfying work situation, we moved to Washington. Our new suburban neighborhood turned out to be a rewarding mixture of many different sorts of people. Most of them were available if needed but out of respect for freedom and privacy were very willing not to bother each other.

Being creatures of their own age, as my children grew they moved toward the freak culture. Part of this involved their being the first kids in our neighborhood to let their hair grow long. So it was that another macho incident came about. One of our neighbors, strong both of will and of muscle, flew the Confederate flag. Otherwise he did not usually insist on displaying his background of being "a good old boy."

One day as the kids were entering their teenage years, someone broke this neighbor's window with a rock. He accused my kids and harassed them. Letting them know that I would stand

140

up for them, I phoned him so that we might talk over the problem. He insisted on coming down the road to our house. I met him on the front steps with my sons. I made clear to him that the boys insisted that they had not broken his window and that I trusted them. I did not believe it was the sort of thing they would lie about. I assured him that if they had done such a thing I would be glad to make restitution and take care of straightening out the kids.

What proof did he have? I demanded. His only answer was that he believed vandalism came out of the ghetto. Ghetto kids had long hair and they broke windows, he insisted. My kids were the only boys in our neighborhood who had long hair. And so he concluded that it must have been one of them who had broken his window.

I made it clear that his reasoning made no sense to me and that I didn't want him to harass my kids anymore. His response was, "If you're gonna be that way, come on out into the road and we'll settle this once and for all!"

I felt very stuck. I didn't want to fight. It seemed needless. I was past being ashamed to back out of a fight. Besides, this guy looked like he could beat my brains out. It was also important to me not to let my kids down. I made a decision on the spot. Forcing down the flush of humiliation, I told him that as far as I was concerned fighting didn't solve anything. I would not go out to the road to fight with him. I also did not want him to harass my kids anymore. He went off shaking his head and muttering disparaging remarks about me.

Old shame (or macho pride) was reawakened by my fear that I had failed in the eyes of my sons. I sat down with the kids and asked them how they felt about my handling of the situation. I feared their contempt. The kids were beautiful. They said that they knew that I loved them. I had stood up for them as a father and they thought it would have been stupid to have fought with this man. My oldest son said that he knew it must have been hard for me to back down from the fight in front of them. He was glad that I had been brave enough to surrender.

For the initially single-dimensional macho male or the equally shallow Southern-belle female, transitional experiences toward acceptance of their androgyny are particularly painful and disruptive. But core changes are difficult for all of us. To ease our way through these transitions we may project onto someone else temporary responsibility for the newly acquired unfamiliar aspect of the self. Typically one female patient reported, "I got so angry at my boyfriend that I finally told him: 'As my therapist would say, "Fuck you!" ' " A young male patient going through his own comparable transition described one experience as having been so upsetting that he told me, "Had I been you I would have cried."

Immersed in that perilous passage between initial recognition and gradual integration of the outer side of our self, we may find projection alone is insufficient to handling the overload. Burdened by the largely unintegrated contrasexual shadow, men become moody and women opinionated. The novice androgyne of either gender may behave like an unconscious parody of the opposite sex.

Newly in contact with the female aspect of his personality, a man may come across as helplessly childlike, irresponsibly self-sorry, contrary, and impractical. Overly sentimental and easily hurt, he becomes an irritably thorny clinging vine. In contrast, a woman newly in touch with her masculine aspect is likely to be hypercritically argumentative and insistently pedantic about unfounded generalizations.

In the arguments that ensue between these couples in transition, the newly assertive woman will attack recklessly with overstatements such as "You never admit when you're wrong." The neophyte male androgyne will respond with petulant accusations about how deeply he is hurt by her unfair attacks. If he can get her to listen, he may subject her to patronizing explanations of "what this is *really* all about."

Self-assertion is the consuming preoccupation of the newly liberated woman. It takes time and practice to get past the many alternately inhibited and exaggerated false starts that inevitably occur in the early stages of transition. As her rage abates, she

142

may be able to begin taking more thoughtful care of her long-neglected self. It will require that she learn to give up mothering the little boy male ego. It will be difficult to do so without losing perspective to understandable bitterness over how much of her self she has already wasted.

During the awkwardly self-conscious shift toward completing her one-sided personality, the woman is likely to pour out a backlog of unexpressed anger in response to even minor frustrations. This female overkill has its reciprocal in the male's equivalent hypersensitivity to even slight bruising of his new-found tender feelings.

Pouty, petulant, and given to tantrums, the tyranically touchy newly androgynous male manages his unfamiliar emotional responsiveness as awkwardly as his female counterpart does her intellectual assertiveness. Neither has yet learned the subtleties that can only be acquired through years of practice. The culture offers no guidance at all in the handling of characteristics traditionally ascribed exclusively to members of the opposite sex.

The woman must actively pursue her masculine aspect, while the man receptively invites his feminine aspect. Apart from that, their situations are equivalent. Whatever aspect of the shadow is being claimed, the development of a more complete self always involves painful inner struggles. When gender is the focus, conflicts inevitably occur not only within the individual but also between the members of the opposite sexes.

In the long run, I still hope it will turn out to be fully worth-while for a man to accept his feminine side and for a woman to accept her masculine aspect. Each will have the opportunity for the richer, freer life afforded by more consciously informed options. The relationship between more androgynous men and women will gradually allow more empathic mutual understanding and respect. But along the way, the transitions will be painfully awkward. They may take more than a single lifetime to complete.

I cannot fault the enlightened goals supported by the human

143

potential and the feminist movements. But no matter how worthwhile their ultimate outcomes, during these times of transition
men and women can be expected to remain understandably un-
forgiving of the encouraged changes in each other.

NOTES, CHAPTER 10

1. Plato, "Symposium," in *The Dialogs of Plato*, vol. I, trans. B. Jowett
(New York; Random House, 1937), pp. 316ff. It is here, in Aristophanes'
discussion of the power of love, that we find the first appearance of androgyny
in classical writings.

2. Virginia Woolf, *Orlando: A Biography* (New York: Harcourt, Brace,
Jovanovich, Harvest Books, 1928).

CHAPTER 11

Your Craziness or Mine?

Going mad can be a terrifying experience. Inner imaginings are mistaken for external events. Fantasy and reality become indistinguishable. Confused by experiences that make no sense, and menaced by reactions that cannot be predicted, the psychotic is often overwhelmed with confusion. Loss of touch with a reality that can be shared with others leaves a person helpless, hopeless, lost, and alone.

But being scared is not the same as being in danger. Tolerance for some craziness can be rewarding. Irrational thoughts may contain unrecognized creative inspirations. Unfettered imaginings can bring vivid color to an otherwise drab, sensibly ordered world. Single-minded sanity soon becomes smug complacency. Insistence on always being realistic and reasonable makes life dull, emptying it of antic fun and wild adventure.

Getting beyond ordinary everyday humdrum sometimes requires the *voluntary* suspension of that disbelieving critical judgment that we usually call "sanity." The altered state of consciousness needed for enriching our experience may depend on willingly going mad from time to time.

Our standards for what is crazy and what is not have been

painfully established. They are not easily suspended. As children we soon learned that behaviors that made our parents mildly uncomfortable were discounted as "silly." Not all *mis*behavior was dismissed so casually. Acts that strongly offended were punished. Some of our transgressions went beyond even that range of controlled parental tolerance. Some upset our parents beyond correction either by dismissal or punishment. Instead, deviations as unthinkable as these were diagnosed. Like other forms of shaming, categorizing some of his or her ways as "crazy" threatens a child with total personal discrediting.

As children, rather than risk the shattering of an acceptable self-image, most of us soon learn to deny just how crazy we can sometimes be. Defensively insisting on our own total sanity, we may grow up harshly judgmental of other people's weird ways. The more single-mindedly sane we become, the more crazies we will find around us. *They* serve as the shadow formed by our projected unacceptable imaginings. Most of our critical diagnostic judgments go unspoken. Some we spit out in arguments as angry accusations. Others are expressed privately as simulated concern in the name of trying to help someone else to behave more sensibly.

As a mental health professional, I was afforded more license than most people for fortifying the denial of my own madness. Early in my career, first as an intern, and later as a staff psychologist, I worked in a section of a state mental hospital segregated to house male criminally insane inmates. In addition to my duties as group therapist for sex offenders, I was regularly assigned the task of diagnostic evaluation of other prisoner/patients. Most of the psychological testing and interviewing I did was part of an in-house effort to classify these inmates and to plan treatment programs during their usually long stay in the hospital.

In some cases, my evaluations helped determine administrative decisions far beyond the scope of the patient's clinical course within the institution. A man might be incarcerated for a short predetermined period of psychiatric observation. The staff's evaluation would later be included in a judicial decision. In these pretrial or presentencing evaluations, my findings regarding the prisoner's psychological condition might well influence a courtroom decision as to his release, his extended incarceration, or possibly even his death by electrocution.[1]

I remember testing Howard, a sweetly boyish, politely reasonable young man who seemed out of place in this building for the criminally insane. In his hometown he had long been known as "a good soul who was a hard worker, read his Bible regular, and never made no trouble."

Before his twenty-eighth birthday, Howard *had* made no trouble. But on the morning of that birthday, he received a visitation revealing that he was to be the Lord's Avenger. In the darkness of his own projected shadow, everywhere he looked, Howard encountered evidence of the sins of others. It took the police only forty-five minutes to disarm this local avenging angel, but by then he had already shot and killed twelve randomly selected sinners and wounded five others. Comfortably detached, Howard told me the whole story without getting upset or expressing remorse. "They shouldn't ought to have done those bad things," he explained.

Howard's religious delusions served as a bastion between his own too-good-to-be-true simple purity of heart and the disowned temptations to sin that he projected onto others. By killing off his shadow, he was able to get his idealized self safely locked away for life without having to recognize that he had ever done anything wrong.

Understandably, Howard's massacre had received extensive media coverage. Sane citizens are fascinated by all the terrible acts that they themselves could never even conceive of committing. Unfortunately, so are some borderland personalities. Uneasily poised between contrivedly compliant surface selves and an underlying core of archaically intense hunger and rage, they are more susceptible to contagion. As a result, in the months that followed, the first massacre set off a minor epidemic of similarly senseless shooting

147

I had a chance to meet one of the young unknown admirers who had set out to emulate Howard. On a subsequent Saturday morning of his own, this barely eighteen-year-old Bobby had taken a rifle and shot everyone in sight. Unlike Howard, Bobby was not detached. Instead, he was terribly upset, but only because he had been unable to match his hero's record of twelve dead and five wounded. Humiliated by the extent of his inadequacy, Bobby admitted that before he was apprehended, he had been able to shoot only three people, none of whom had even died. But the final blow came only after Bobby had arrived at the building for the criminally insane. It was there he learned from the other inmates that his hero had become "nothing but a jailhouse fag-punk."

Psychotics sometimes act out the forbidden fantasies of saner, more stable citizens. Only a rare marginal personality will publicly claim a certified lunatic as a hero, but even though the larger community denounces the mad pariah, still the "fiend" may serve as secret proxy for some of these sane-seeming critics.

One clear example comes to mind. A man I will call John set fire to a cathedral, unintentionally killing a monsignor. The liberal-minded psychiatric staff members showed a curious sympathy toward John's crime. The fact that it was a church that he had burned and a priest that he had killed often elicited the sort of nervous kidding that supported the wry observation that "anti-Catholicism is the anti-Semitism of the liberals."

The week following my testing of John I did a psychodiagnostic evaluation of a man who insisted on being called Pravda (the Russian word for *truth*). In his own flamboyant way, this second madman acknowledged his hatred of the Catholic church more openly than the staff members. He told a long delusional tale of his having been banished to another planet almost two thousand years ago. Originally he was the anti-Christ. More recently, following the degeneration of Christianity through the Reformation, Bolshevik Marxism, and Sexual Modernism, he had been summoned out of exile. By destroying the now-decadent Visible Catholic Church he was to restore the pristine purity of the

Invisible True Christian Church. As proof of his sacred mission, Pravda showed me his stigmata. He admitted that the marks on his hands and on his forehead were scratches suffered during a hurried climb over a barbed-wire fence while trying to escape from the police. At the same time, he insisted that they were also the scars of wounds inflicted by his crucifiers when they crowned him with thorns and nailed him to the cross.

Through the grapevine, Pravda had learned that I had interviewed John the previous week. The first thing he wanted to know was, "When you spoke to John, did he confess to starting the cathedral fire that killed the monsignor?" I told him that I was no more free to discuss with him what John had told me than I would be to tell other patients anything that he might reveal. "OK, OK, I understand," Pravda replied. "But just for the record, if John says he didn't burn that church, then I confess that I did it!" I felt less confused by mad Pravda's honest attitudes toward John's crazy crime than by the saner comments of my liberal colleagues.

My involvement with Pravda was restricted to that one psychological testing session and the report of my findings that became part of his clinical chart. John, on the other hand, was one of the patient/prisoners on whose behalf I was subpoenaed to testify as an expert witness.

His history revealed that he had started out as an unassumingly marginal member of one of many close-knit small self-segregated ethnic subcultures within a large New Jersey city. John had passively bumbled along for most of his life without creating any significant disturbance. Although it was long clear that he was peculiar and inept, he had never been considered dangerous. The people who had known him from childhood comfortably tolerated his strange ways. They saw to it that enough paid work was available for him to be able to make his own way and to maintain his pride. Within this familiar, sympathetic neighborhood setting of large allowances and small demands, with a little help from his friends, he managed to live insignificantly.

Though not unintelligent, John had always been "slow." Responding from earliest childhood to others' insistence that he "take it easy" and not "make trouble," he soon learn to hide his intense emotional turmoil beneath a false shell of seeming indifference and mock retardation. As in the rest of his development, John was also slow in showing romantic interest in women. Whatever his secret longings, it was not until his late twenties that John attempted a courtship. The object of his affection was an outsider, a young woman who only came to John's neighborhood to work. From his naive account, it sounded to me as though she had accepted his attentions without ever really caring about him. Perhaps the superficial flattery of his entreaties filled some private emptiness within her. Maybe she simply wanted to exploit her adoring dummy. In any case, for a while she allowed John's courtship.

Encouraged by her acceptance, John grew more insistent. Though they had never even kissed, he began talking about their "setting the date." The young woman told John that she liked him a lot, but regrettably she could never "get serious" with him. She did not understand his peculiarly vague Protestant upbringing. Unless he was willing to convert to her own Roman Catholicism, they would have no future. In recounting his beloved's demand, John still believed her sincerely willing to marry him if only he converted. To me it sounded more like she was simply attempting to discourage his more aggressive attentions.

Without hesitation John had agreed to convert. He would do anything she wished. For a little while he was happy in the belief that he could easily make the gesture of good faith that she asked of him. John had no idea that there would be any more required of him than verbal agreement to become a Catholic. He knew that he would probably have to attend services at the cathedral some Sundays, but he had no idea that he would have to "take instruction." He had always been slow in school, marginally making his way on the basis of unearned social promotions. When he learned that the conversion process would involve more of the studying and examinations that had always made him feel so inadequate, John was terribly upset.

But John was also terribly in love and so he tried, and he tried, and he tried. I have no idea just how the situation was viewed by the priest who gave John instruction. He may have thought that his pupil could master the material, and he would someday marry his "girl friend" in the church. I only know that John came to feel that, no matter how hard he tried, he would never be able to "pass instruction." After a time, rage smoldered beneath the frustration of his inept efforts. Unable to direct his anger toward the young woman, John became incensed at the church for subjecting him to what he experienced as humiliation. It was not his girl friend's fault that he was unhappy. She only wanted him to be a Catholic like her. The church could have just said OK, but for some reason that John could not figure out, they just wouldn't do it. Instead they made him study a lot of stupid stuff that just made him seem even dumber than he was.

John was getting madder and madder. It was frightening. His place in the community had always depended on his not getting angry with anyone. He knew that if he took out his frustration on the priest he would get into big trouble. The Roman Catholic church and its doctrine were abstract beyond John's comprehension. He needed a clearer, more concrete target for his rage. He had never dared direct his anger openly toward another human being. In the past, he had sometimes solved such problems by secretly burning some small possession stolen from his frustrators.

After some confused deliberations, John settled on the cathedral itself as the object of his retaliation. This church building was the site where the degrading ordeals of instruction had taken place. Located well beyond the sheltering boundaries of the neighborhood that had served as a lifelong haven, it seemed in another world. If the cathedral had stood within his home territory, he could not have burned it down.

I believe that John told the truth when he swore that he thought the cathedral was empty when he set fire to it. Certainly, he would have had no way of knowing of the late-night presence of the monsignor who died in the fire. John was unprepared for arrest and bewildered to find himself charged with murder.

Awaiting trial, he was housed temporarily in the building for the criminally insane. During his ninety-day period of psychiatric observation, he was referred twice to the psychology department for psychodiagnostic testing. The first examination was conducted just after John had arrived at the hospital. At that time, he was deeply disturbed, confused, and somewhat disoriented. Psychiatric observations over the next several weeks indicated that he seemed less and less crazy. Because of these changes, it was decided that he was stable enough to be scheduled for his day in court. Because shifts in his behavior suggested that he was emerging from his acute psychotic episode, further assessment was indicated. John was referred to the psychology department for a follow-up evaluation. This time I assigned the task to one of the psychology interns, restricting my own role to supervising the report of the test results.

When John went to trial, the defense subpoenaed my testimony as an expert witness. Never having appeared in court before, my mood alternated between the mild high of being an officially acknowledged expert and the awful feeling that I didn't know anything. Once I had been sworn in on the witness stand, the prosecuting attorney did all he could to discredit my expertise and to publicly substantiate my private doubts about knowing anything at all. From my precarious perch on the witness stand, he seemed like a cobra. Lulling me with his soft tones and simulated reverence, again and again he would quickly shift into harshly discrediting disclaimers.

The prosecutor knew from the beginning that I had not yet completed my Ph.D. Repeatedly he addressed me as if, for the moment, he had forgotten. Each time with mock remorse he corrected himself: "Now I'd like to ask you something else, *Doctor*. Oh, I *am* sorry. You haven't completed your training to be a doctor, have you *Mister* Kopp?"

He baited me to discredit my findings just as he had to disqualify my credentials. Wanting so to be taken seriously as a sage, I was easily seduced by his inviting me to explain just how the Rorschach test was used as a psychodiagnostic instrument. When I had finished, just to make sure that he (and the jury) understood, with simulated seriousness the prosecutor summarized what I had said. Gradually his voice tone shifted from awed reverence to stunned disbelief. Finally, he undid my entire presentation with a single simple question: "Mr. Kopp, are you trying to tell this court that you can know someone's secret thoughts, and that you can decide whether or not he is crazy, just by asking him to tell you what a bunch of accidental inkblots look like to him?"

By this time I was not making much sense, even to myself. A few times the defense attorney had objected to the prosecutor's derision of my testimony. Each time the prosecutor offered sufficient justification for the judge to overrule the objection. Were it not for the judge's anxiety about whether or not he himself was crazy, my findings would have been completely discredited.

As I explained the Rorschach's evocation of fantasies, the judge looked more and more intrigued. At one point he broke in to tell me that years and years ago he had studied psychology in college. The mere exposure to that subject matter had churned up many of his own fantasies, making him wonder if he himself was crazy. Controlling the desperation in his voice he interrupted the prosecutor to ask me for reassurance: "Everybody who studies psychology has fantasies and worries a little bit about whether or not he's crazy. Isn't that right? That's *normal*, isn't it?"

The judge's turning to me for an opinion was in itself reassuring. Additionally, it was a relief to answer a question without worrying that it might be a trap. And so with great sympathy and assumed authority, I reassured the judge that what he had described was "completely normal." A few minutes later when I was testifying about John's intelligence test findings, the judge expressed his gratitude by officially validating my expert status. At the time of John's first testing he was so upset and bewildered that his IQ score was only 80. Recognizing that his poor func-

tioning and seeming dullness was a function of temporary confusion and emotional turmoil, I reported (and testified) that he
showed potential for average intelligence under optimal circumstances. Interrupting the prosecutor's assault on my integrity,
the judge pointed out that my *earlier* prediction of John's potential for average intelligence had been *scientifically* proven by
his scoring an IQ of *exactly* 100 on the second testing.

By trading reassurances with one another, the judge and I
had each quieted any doubts about our own sanity. I had diagnosed his fears as "normal." He, in turn, had judged my findings
"scientific." We had bonded together in this microcosm of the
larger community, promising one another, "I'll acknowledge
your good sense if you'll acknowledge mine." That distorted
mirroring was necessary but not sufficient to the disavowal of
any personal craziness in either of us. Like any self-satisfied
in-group, we also needed outcasts with whom to contrast ourselves. Professionally, I got to evaluate crazies who were sometimes criminal. He got to judge criminals who were sometimes
crazy.

It is just this sort of mutual support in defining ourselves as
sane and others as crazy that encourages professional helpers to
be smugly unaware of how we scapegoat the deviants we profess
to serve. As double agents, too often we betray our commitments
to the needy outcasts in favor of our loyalty to the community
on whom we depend for our own validation.

But complacency and disloyalty are not the only hazards of
insisting that our own good sense is beyond question. Psychological equilibrium demands that the supersane seek out very
crazy partners onto whom their own dark madness can be projected. With this reassurance comes the danger that once drawn
into the shadow of the Double we may find ourselves no longer
able to tell just which one of us is crazy.

The mistaken belief that we can exploit madness in another
without being touched by it in ourselves is chillingly explored
in Truman Capote's "The Headless Hawk."[2] This short story
tells of a complacently realistic young man who sometimes
"wondered why it was that eccentricity always excited in him

154

such curious admiration. It was the feeling he'd had as a child toward carnival freaks. And it was true that about those whom he'd loved there was always a little something wrong, broken."[3]

The story begins on a late winter afternoon in New York City. Leaving the art gallery that he manages, Vincent encounters a strange young woman on the street. Like a lost child, she does not seem to know where she is going. She follows him home, but Vincent enters his apartment alone, trying to think no more about her.

A few days later the young woman shows up at the gallery. She carries a wrapped picture she has painted that she would like him to buy. Simultaneously confused and excited by her somewhat incoherent explanations, he encourages her to unwrap the canvas. It turns out to be a crude painting, "a headless figure in a monklike robe reclined complacently on top of a tacky vaudeville trunk; in one hand she held a fuming blue candle, in the other a miniature gold cage, and her severed head lay bleeding at her feet, . . . the wings of a hawk headless, scarlet-breasted, copper-clawed, curtained the background like a night-fall sky."[4]

Responding to the bizarre painting with an inner sense of recognition, Vincent buys the painting and takes it home to hang over his mantle. For months he expects the young woman to reappear. Knowing only that she refers to herself as "D.J." and that she sometimes stays at the YWCA, he cannot find her. With her image haunting his imagination, Vincent is so uncharacteristically preoccupied that his friends assume that he must be in love.

That spring, in a penny arcade, Vincent accidentally meets her again. This time, he asks her to come home with him. Her answer, when it comes, is a whispered, "Please." On the way home, he is unable even to make conversation with her. D.J. is compliant but unresponsive. When finally she speaks it is of times and places with which he is unfamiliar, and of connections that he cannot understand. As in their first incoherent encounter, she refers repeatedly to a Mr. Destronelli, as if it is a name that

155

everyone must know. Pressed for an explanation, she can only say, "Well, he looks like you, like me, like most anybody."

She yields easily to Vincent's insistence that she stay. Without appearing to know exactly where she is, nor how long she has been there, D.J. moves in to stay with Vincent as his lover. Somehow she seems to believe that she is there because of Mr. Destronelli. When Vincent tries to tell her that she is there because he loves her, she demands to know what became of the others to whom he told that.

Vincent sees their arrangement as an ideal setup. Asking nothing in return, D.J. submits to Vincent's every wish. Unfortunately, she cannot cook. Mostly they eat at her favorite restaurant, the Automat. At least in that tawdry setting she does not look out of place in the violet-adorned leather windbreaker that she wears whenever she leaves the house. Vincent tries to ignore her strange appearance, her odd ways, and her bizarre remarks, but he realizes that he cannot reveal to friends his explotive relationship with this crazy lady.

Gradually attachment to D.J. isolates him more and more. The crazier she gets, the more Vincent withdraws from his usual contacts. The role of keeper can also become a full-time job. As she becomes more openly delusional, Vincent can no longer ignore his terror that she may someday kill him.

Finally, he decides that the only way of putting her out of his life is to sneak away alone on a long vacation. After secretly arranging for his trip, Vincent sends D.J. off to the Automat one last time. While she is out he packs his own bags to take to the airport. Then he packs her seedy cardboard suitcase, leaving it outside of the locked door of his apartment.

Apart from D.J. at last, for the first time in months Vincent feels safe and sane. After staying away long enough to be sure that he has escaped her, he looks forward to returning to New York. He wants to resume the normal life he had known before he met her, to be able once more to entertain his friends and to accept their invitations. For a while, he is free of her madness, living as sensibly as he had before he met her.

Then one evening months later, Vincent is out walking the dark streets. He pauses under a lamppost. Cardboard suitcase in hand, like a homeless child, D.J. appears under the street light. Trustingly, she stands beside him without speaking. It is clear that Vincent will never again escape her craziness.

In some families, one member is expected to carry and contain the craziness that all the rest of them might otherwise have to acknowledge as their own. The supersane parents often insist that except for the identified patient, everyone else in the family is "completely normal."

Early in my career I was invited to serve as an occasionally participating observer in a radically imaginative family therapy configuration of these sane/crazy people. Each session began with thirteen of us distributed unevenly around the perimeter of a group meeting room. Each of the families sat in a separate triangular cluster. Further isolated, the parents sat side by side, rarely facing each other, never touching. Completing each isosceles triangle sat the young adult schizophrenic son or daughter about whom the parents fretted. Randomly interspersed between families sat four psychotherapists.

In such families, it is not unusual for the grown child to have become psychotic at a time when he or she would otherwise have left the parents to fend for themselves in dealing with each other. During the course of therapy the work often focused on this collusion of seemingly sane parents and their obviously crazy kids. Over a period of many, many months a transformation began to occur in the destructively intradependent family configurations.

During the family group meetings, the younger generation had established an increasingly dependable exchange of peer support. A beginning sense of separation from the original triads was allowed by this cross-family support. This independence was further bolstered by individual therapy sessions in which each young person could count on a therapeutic alliance with a counselor of his or her own. Slowly, we began to see the beginnings of their individuation into separate selves. Psychosis

157

had too long served as an alternative to overdue phase-appropriate need for a life apart from their parents.

The emergence of one of these young psychotics stands out particularly in my memory, perhaps because her gaining an uncontaminated separate self so clearly pivoted on returning to her father the craziness he had assigned to her care. When the family group sessions first began, Mary's eventual willowy grace was prefigured only as a wraithlike unworldliness. During those first few sessions she was openly crazy most of the time. When some participation was asked of her, she remained sullenly mute. Only when her parents seemed to be making contact with one another would Mary break her silence to launch into a loud, rambling religious diatribe. These semicoherent sermonettes usually centered on chastity as the only protection against eternal damnation. Essential to her thesis were the revelations she had received when God appeared to her. It was His voice that had announced that she was the new Virgin Mary, chosen to bear the second Christ.

From the beginning, Mary's parents seemed to ignore how crazy she acted. They did, however, express continuing concern about her chronically poor physical posture and her often unkempt appearance. Father was as stolidly sane as his daughter was crazy. This superbright computer expert was almost always detached and intellectual, reserving emotional intensity for self-righteous displays of prudery. Mary's mother was a saintly soul who seemed ready to sacrifice her own personal needs to a life of full-time service as her daughter's keeper and her husband's handmaiden.

The changes in Mary surfaced earlier than those in her parents. With the support of the other young people, she had begun to pay attention to living a life of her own. As she developed independent, secular interests she became livelier, prettier. During a family group session she announced that she had gotten a job. What's more, she planned to move out of her parents' home and into an apartment of her own.

The other young people and some of the therapists delightedly encouraged her progress. Only Mary's parents seemed upset.

After so long ignoring her bizarre behavior, they now began expressing concern about her ability to take proper care of herself. "After all," they insisted, "we all know how crazy Mary is."

Mary insisted that she had changed. "I know now that when we first began therapy I was really crazy. I was afraid of sex, maybe even afraid of life. I truly believed that God had chosen me. Now I understand that was only my fantasy. Those weren't heavenly voices I heard. They were all just part of the craziness in my head."

Understandably upset by the prospect of his daughter's going sane, Mary's father abandoned his characteristic detachment. Visibily shaken, he launched a tearful emotional protest against his daughter's newfound sanity. "Deny not our Lord," he pleaded. "You can't be sure that what you've heard was just mental." Encouraged by his wife, he went on to cite scriptural validation for the religious reality of God's speaking directly to souls specially chosen for their purity. He urged that Mary not turn away from her calling lest she experience temptations of corruption of the flesh and risk eternal damnation. Though he never referred explicitly to her sacred virginal state, his proscription was clear.

The primary therapist challenged father's destructive need to keep Mary crazy. The other young people joined to support Mary's somewhat shaky stand against her father's usually unquestioned domination. By the following week, Mary was more solidly sure of her own good sense, but her father showed up for the session crazier than before.

It was now father to whom God had personally spoken. He was instructed to undertake a holy crusade against psychotherapy. God instructed that he begin by reporting back to the referring minister just how therapy corrupted religious revelations by reducing them to hallucinations. In a rambling, occasionally incoherent tirade, he repeated the denunciation, which ended up directly focused on the senior therapist: "I told my minister all about your scandalous blaspheming ways. You're in big trouble now. You'll never have another Christian family referred to you. I even sent word to the bishop that you are a perverted destroyer of the faith, you and all the other Jewish Communist shrinks!"

During this mad denunciation by the now crazy father, the senior therapist only smiled silently. When the man's rage was finally spent, the therapist answered only, "Tattletale!"

Father had irrevocably exposed as his own the burden of craziness usually carried by his daughter. The therapist's playful response defused the crisis long enough to begin examination of this destructive game of musical madness. In group it became clearer how each family depended on displaced craziness to maintain a system in which individual members could allow unacceptable aspects of their individual selves to remain unexplored.

Driving one member of a family crazy is an extreme solution to dealing with the divided self. Most of us go through life without getting stuck in either of the reciprocal roles of crazy or keeper. Most even escape suffering the extremes of vertical, horizontal, or biased personality splitting. Even so, we all find ourselves divided by the inevitable internal contradictions between self-expression and conventional morality, as well as by those inherent in our androgyny, in our choosing between reason and imagination, and between our wishes to merge and yet to retain our separate identities.

NOTES, CHAPTER 11

1. At that time, some capital criminals were still executed in the electric chair at the Trenton State Prison. This threat added to the professional staff members' need to assure themselves that they had nothing in common with the homicidal maniacs. The desperation of our detachment was expressed with grotesque clarity in the sentiments of one particularly callous staff psychologist named George. Though we had all been invited to witness the next execution, only George had agreed to attend. The day before his scheduled electrocution, the condemned prisoner managed to get a stay of execution. When George learned of the prisoner's successful appeal, his only response was: "Party pooper!"

2. Truman Capote, "The Headless Hawk," in *The Grass Harp and a Tree of Night and Other Stories* (New York: New American Library, Signet Book, 1951), pp. 175–195.

3. Ibid., p. 179.

4. Ibid., pp. 179–180.

PART IV
All of Me

Nothing human is alien to me.
—Terence,
Heautontimoroumenos

CHAPTER 12

Another Whom We Do Not Know

In the long run, every personality is divided. Even those children who grew up in near-optimal circumstances of safety, support, and care are subject to some disavowal of parts of the self. Though not as extreme or as comprehensive as pathological splitting off, the everyday variety also offers protection, and always at a price.

The cost is higher in the more pervasive pathological splitting, but lesser instances of the seeming peculiarities of psychopathology are evident in all of us. It is for this reason that the ways in which neurotics and character disorders disavow aspects of themselves can be instructive to the less dramatically damaged majority of people. "Patients" are just like everyone else, *only more so*. So, too, the ways that therapy helps those of us who have been more seriously damaged can serve as a guide to self-acceptance for the less divided, everyday personalities.

But before our self-acceptance can be expanded, we must first heighten our awareness of what it feels like to have a self. The boundary between what is self and what is not-self is more than an abstract conceptual distinction. The boundaries of the self

[163]

can be experienced on a very primitive level. This is clearest when attention is focused on the inside/outside boundaries of the body that contains (or sometimes "is") the self.

Most of the time, I am not "self-conscious" of either the psychological "me" nor of its physical aspect. But whenever the boundaries of either one are challenged, I can become uncomfortably aware of the distinction between which contents are acceptable and which are not. The subtly shifting interplay at the semipermeable membrane that bounds the self is thrown into boldest relief when I am threatened with feeling violated by having to admit (or admit to) contents that do not seem to belong within my self-image.

On the physical level, the "true" boundaries of my physical self are portrayed metaphorically in "my spittin' image." Usually, I pay no attention to my own saliva. I take it for granted as a natural part of my internal physical self. Should I discover a bad taste or a foreign substance in my mouth, I may "spit it out." At such times, I am careful where I spit. Curiously, this constraint is not restricted to the original foreign substance. The same saliva that a moment ago seemed comfortably acceptable inside of my mouth becomes "dirty" as soon as my spitting makes it seem a part of the outside world. Should I "drool" a bit of spittle, I am embarrassed by my involuntary loss of control over what remains inside myself. If I take a drink, once inside my mouth the water mixes with my saliva. Knowing that what I swallow is a mixture of the two doesn't make me feel less refreshed. But what if, for some reason, I should spit into the glass of water? The idea of drinking that mixture seems immediately distasteful. Inside my body, that same saliva seemed a natural part of me. Once outside it has now become so foreign that it contaminates the water that was pure enough to drink only a moment ago. Spoiled by saliva that is no longer mine, the water has now become unfit to be included as part of my physical self.

In reality, neither the water nor the saliva has changed. It is only my conception of these substances that has changed. It

164

is not my actual physical self to which they have become unacceptable. It is only my *image* of that physical self that would be violated by my drinking that spit-soiled glass of water.

There is no way to know what we *really* are. All we can know is a self-concept. This image is not the "real self"; rather, it is a *picture* of the self, a composite of our best wishes and of our worst fears about who we really are.

Everyone has a self-concept. Its public aspect is likely to be made up of the more desirable qualities (whether actual or imagined). This more acceptable image is the one that we are most comfortable presenting to other people. It is tempting to take this idealization as the true representation of who we are.

From the beginning of our lives, we each live in a world that is only imperfectly suited to our individual needs. We must learn to accommodate, or we must die. Emotional survival is, in large measure, a matter of maintaining self-esteem. Unless we feel good enough about who we are, life doesn't seem worth living.

At times, our "looking-glass self"[1] is the only source of good feelings about who we are. No matter how bad we feel privately, we may be able to maintain a social self-image that feels acceptable. This image is not necessarily the way others really see us. Rather, it is a reflection of how we imagine they see us.

Each of us must manage the contradictions between this more worthy public aspect of the self and its often more questionably valued hidden underside. Some of the qualities that are relegated to the private aspect may seem so unacceptable to the idealized self that they must be ignored, denied, or disowned.[2] Relegating this side to the shadows saves us from awareness of intolerably self-denigrating feelings of shame and guilt. Unfortunately, some of these awful secrets are so threatening to our self-esteem that we may hide them not only from others' gaze, but from our own awareness as well. Ironically, we risk others' knowing our failings better than we do. It may be only ourselves that we fool. Worse yet, qualities that we try so hard to hide might turn out to be more acceptable to others. Some people may love us without demanding that we be something other than what we are.

For much of my own life, harsh self-judgments have needlessly divided my personality. Too often I yield to the temptation to display as authentic an image that is actually a misleadingly flattering, touched-up formal portrait. *Posing as myself* robs me of spontaneity and minimizes new experiences. How often I have settled for nothing more than another petty moral victory. At such times all I do is convince myself that once more I was right to have concealed my vulnerability! I have successfully avoided risking lowering my self-esteem, but only at the cost of missing any possibility of increasing my feelings of worth. Security for the one requires sacrificing opportunity for the other.

Under certain circumstances, I may have no other option but to divide myself. But even well-warranted disavowal of parts of myself has its price. Like all other internal security operations, the bastions of the divided self often require constraints disproportionate to the safety they provide.

Like you, too often I have ended up having to juggle too many selves. Life sometimes seems a poorly constructed bedroom farce, providing more embarrassment than entertainment. Unless we learn to live with some of the contradictions between our revealed and our concealed selves, lack of consistency makes our personal identities seem fraudulent, our experiences unreal, and our lives meaningless.

The world is not set up to meet all of our needs. No one else sees us as the center of the universe. Accommodating to life's disinterested, imperfect fit requires doing what significant others expect of us. In learning to appear to be what the mothering ones seem to want us to be, we must constrain unfitting behavior. Though we disguise our true motives with the mask of a false self, we retain hidden incongruent private thoughts, feelings, and wishes. We learn to act one way for others to see, all the while knowing that this performance is not the real self. But like all things demonic, the false self that we develop as a strategy of deliberate deception can get out of hand. After a while the lies we tell begin to seem true. The false self may end up becoming the only reality we know.

166

At the outset, the false self is contrived as an accommodation to those on whom we depend for nurturance. In addition, this masquerade also serves to protect the anonymity of the true self. This pretense sets up an uneasy balance. If the mask is an effective enough disguise, the true face beneath it is allowed a secret life of its own. If too effective, the false face of compliance ends up becoming our only available identity. We cannot wear this mask without the risk of giving up our own personal way of life.

In the beginning, when a child is small and helplessly dependent, pretending provides a much-needed sense of power. But this deception can become a dangerous game of hide-and-seek in which *"it is a joy to be hidden but a disaster not to be found."*[3]

The world is sometimes kind, often harsh, and ultimately indifferent to our personal needs. In order to survive, each of us has had to learn to accommodate to some of the expectations of the individuals and the community on whom we depend. Pretense is everywhere, but it need not be all there is. Pathological division of a personality sacrifices opportunity for being the true self. In the end, pathologically split personalities often end up leading completely false lives. When not acting out the contrived role of the false self, they are at a loss to know what else they might be.

It is not the pretending that discredits the authenticity of their lives. It is *pretending that they are not pretending* that transforms the false self into antiself. Behavioral strategies originally contrived to fool others become self-deceptions. Eventually, the pretender no longer knows who he or she really is.

When the pretending is no longer conscious, the false self has ceased to operate as an agent of the true self. As a double agent, the antiself betrays the true self. In any case, there is no escape. Whatever is ignored within the self will surely be encountered in the outside world. The projected parts of ourselves begin to appear in our experiences of other people. We are all filled with contradictions. Those that we cannot accept as existing within

167

us are fated to be encountered as happening to us from outside. During any given day, each of us is exposed to a projected kaleidoscope of the unaccepted parts of ourselves. Each instance will be experienced as an emotionally charged glimpse of another person. These brief encounters with our projections can be identified by the short-lived overvalent reactions each is sure to evoke in us. Whether pleasant or painful, these experiences are always unwarrantedly disruptive.

Some of these projections are more long-lasting. Every relationship has some element of Laurel and Hardy reciprocal projections. If not disproportionate, there is even psychological wisdom in seeking out partners who provide elements that we cannot find within ourselves. It is often our enthrallment with the exquisite differences offered by our "better half" that provides both the richness and the pain of long-term love relationships.

In the case of pathologically divided personalities, most of the significant relationships are no more than shadow dances. In their chronic marriages, feuds, and other good guy/bad guy melodramas, the other partner serves largely as an exploited alter ego, a container for the unacceptable qualities that have been split off from the self. When too much of the relationship is a product of projection, we end up with grotesque stereotypes of the detached obsessional male wedded to the labile hysterical female, the saint and the sinner, the Neanderthal and the nun, the good spouse of the bad souse, and so on. But every encounter with a projection is an opportunity for greater self-awareness. We often ignore what they can teach us, but always at our hazard.

A particularly macabre tale of the shadow dance of a false self and his deadly Double is told by Tennessee Williams. "Desire and the Black Masseur"[4] introduces Anthony Burns as having suffered neglect in a family of fifteen children in which he was the one given least notice. Early on he learned to sacrifice the autonomy of a separate personal self: "From his very beginning this person had betrayed an instinct for being included in things that swallowed him up, and still he did not feel secure."[5] After graduating from a very large high-school class, he secured a position as a clerk in the largest wholesale company of the city. When he was not working, Burns loved to sit in the back rows of movie theaters absorbed by the darkness and swallowed up in the crowd. But none of his ways of hiding out in the shadows fully satisfied him. Timidly, he shuttled from one kind of protection to another.

At the age of thirty, Burns still had the unformed look of a child moving in the presence of critical elders. It was as if he were apologizing for the little space he had selected to occupy. Unaware of his own desires, he lacked curiosity, interest, or specific longing. He seemed left with only one basic longing. Again and again, he was driven to immerse his insufficiency in the shadows that might complete his unfinished self. Ever guided by others' needs, he lived by the principal of atonement. All he came to desire for himself was "surrender . . . to violent treatment by others with the idea of thereby clearing . . . (his) self of . . . guilt." Unconsciously he sought punishment for sins he could not even imagine committing. Without conscious attention or effort, he discovered the Double who would become the instrument of his atonement.

Burns suffered from low back pain. Massage had been recommended. Despite his shyness, he felt compelled to visit a Turkish bath. Unconscious desire outwitted defensive denial and timidity. Almost without knowing what he was doing, he went to the baths that Saturday afternoon.

The baths turned out to offer a surprisingly assuring atmosphere of secrecy and concealment. Patrons were almost as white as the loose tentlike sheaths that covered their moist barefooted figures. The masseurs were all blacks. "Dark and positive against the loose white hangings of the baths. They wore no sheets, they had on loose cotton drawers, and they moved about with force and resolution."[6] Compared to the apologetic whispering of the patrons, the boldness of their voices made it clear that they alone had authority here.

Burns stood even more uncertainly than most of the uneasy patrons. Though he had paid the price of a bath and massage, for a time he stood around not knowing what to do. Soon the black masseur came and propelled him into one of the curtained compartments. "Take off your clothes." Naked at the direction of the black, he was given a white sheet to put on. All of this took place in the heat, moisture, and misty white vapor of the steam bath. Grateful for the temporary envelopment, he followed where the black led.

"Lie on the table." Burns obeyed. Pouring alcohol on the middle of the patron's soft belly, the black began the massage with a terrific whack. Flipping him over, the masseur increased the violence of his blows to the shoulders and buttocks. As the violence and pain increased, so did the pleasure. "So by surprise is a man's desire discovered, and once discovered, the only need is surrender. . . ."[7]

The masseur "hated white-skinned bodies because they abused his pride. He loved to have their white skin thrown beneath him. . . ."[8] All that he had longed for he found in this clerk. When apart, they dreamed of each other and they understood how they completed one another. One searched for atonement, and the other for an object of redeeming punishment.

The violence between them increased. One day Burns left the bath with two cracked ribs. Each time the damage was worse. During one massage, when the masseur broke his leg, Burns was unable to stifle his outcry. The manager came and threw them both out. The masseur carried his partner to a room in the black section of town.

Here they resumed and continued their passion for a week. "You know what you have to do now?" the victim asked. Nodding, the black giant "picked up the body, which barely held together, and placed it gently on a clean-swept table."[9] The giant began the merger of the two shadow half selves. It took him twenty-four hours. The story ends with the black sucking clean the white bones that are all that is left of Burns.

We all project onto other people those personal qualities that

170

we do not accept as our own. Few of our projections are as consuming as Burns. Still, because the people onto whom we direct our projections often are exactly what we see them to be, it can be very difficult to tell where they end and we begin.

The less pathological the divisions within our own personalities, the more likely that we will project our disavowed assertiveness onto a truly aggressive person, our denied indolence onto someone who is truly casual, and our disowned sensuality onto someone who really does indulge in physical pleasures. Distinguishing the extent of projection in our perceptions requires our paying attention to disproportionate emotional reactions they evoke in us. When we are *not* projecting, we can observe the personal characteristics of others free of moralistic condemnation, worshipful admiration, or enthralling fascination. If we *are* projecting, we are likely to fault the assertive person for being "domineering," to criticize the casual type for being "lazy and ineffectual," or to accuse the sensualist of being a "moral degenerate." Even given these emotional indications, to some extent we will be left wondering how much of what we experience in these interactions belongs to us and how much to objects of our projection.

Fortunately, our store of available projections is not restricted to this amalgam of ambiguously distorted daytime experiencing of other people. In dreams our projections are available to us in purer form. During our waking hours, the extent of our projections is obscured by the contribution of other people's own psychic productions. The private uncluttered space of dreams provides clearer reflections of our darker sides. If we pay attention, they can serve as a dark mirror to our waking consciousness, clearly revealing those aspects of ourselves that we have relegated to the obscurity of our shadows. These disowned parts of the self are projected in the form of all the other people, things and events that appear in our dreams.[10]

Recently, Sidney, a young man whom I see in therapy, was struggling against beginning awareness of long-repressed rage. Understandably, he was frightened of its release. Because of

171

their own projections, Sidney's parents had always imagined his anger as being dangerous. Early on théy had coerced him into relegating this aspect of his nature to the darkness of the unconscious.

This primary repression was compounded further by the splitting off of any character traits earthy and hardy enough to be congruent with his rage. Programmed to be a sweet, sensitive, ineffectual boy, Sidney had learned to renounce any attitude his mother might have experienced as gross or inconsiderate, along with any show of force that his father might interpret as an expression of rebellion. All of this primary horizontal division of personality was elegantly elaborated by further splitting on a hysterical bias. By the time I met Sidney, he had long since learned to cherish the uncomfortably proper postures demanded by his parents. His air of superiority, his sterile detachment, and his somewhat effeminate elegance had all come to seem natural to him. The rage he had so long ago set aside remained imprisoned in the decorative cage of his hysterical false self. Though Sidney could feel the turmoil stirring within, he was reluctant to risk polluting his image of elegance by exposure to the raw crude power beneath the shiny veneer.

During this period of hesitation at the edge of darkness, Sidney reported a dream heavy with projections of unrecognized aspects of himself. Our examination of his dream expanded his awareness of the force of his underlying rage. More important, the dream's unconscious mockery of Sidney's hysteria challenged his conscious valuing of this neurotically theatrical posturing. For the first time, his very identity was brought into question. If the core of who he was turned out to be someone quite different from the false self created to please his parents, then who would he be . . . really?

On the afternoon preceding the night of Sidney's dream, the news media had been dominated by storm warnings. It was the first hurricane season affected by the feminist movement, the first time that these natural disasters were free of traditionally sexist designations. Alternate storms had been named David

172

and Frederick. Perhaps someday a storm might be named Sidney. That, in a sense, was Sidney's dream.

He introduced his account of the dream by telling me: "I'd been listening to the storm warnings all day. Usually that sort of thing doesn't faze me. But now it's different. I suppose it has to do with my becoming aware of stormy feelings somewhere inside me. At any rate, it took me a long time to fall asleep that night.

"The dream began with my hearing storm warnings wherever I turned. It was like being here in therapy. Nowadays no matter what I begin talking about, in the end I discover that I'm about to get terribly angry and upset.

"In the dream, I was a caretaker. My job was to protect all the breakable decorative pieces in the house from storm damage by moving them away from the windows. Mainly, I was concerned with looking after the good china and the smoked glass objets d'art that my mother so cherishes.

"The pieces that stick in my mind are a set of blue colored glasses. They are exactly the sort of unique, exotic *chotchkas*[11] that she and I would consider especially beautiful, the *crème de la crème*. Oddly enough, in the dream I remember thinking that they seemed more like gaudy kitsch. So much effort had gone into making them unusual that they ended up looking misshapen. They were too fragile to be of any practical use at all. And someone had overdecorated them so with hand-painted yellow pansies that to me they looked grotesque."

Sidney completed his account of the dream by adding, "When it came to taking care of my own room, all I could think of was making my bed. That's when I woke up."

I remained silent. He went on to say, "I remembered that in the past we found that often I woke up just when a dream threatened to confront me with something about myself that I didn't want to know."

At this point Sidney seemed stuck. I encouraged his going on by saying, "This time, you woke from the dream just as you were protecting yourself from the storm by making up your bed."

He responded with a tone of self-disgust. "It made sense in the dream, but now it seems like a pretty stupid way of preparing to weather the storm. It reminds me of my mother's insistence that I always make sure that the underwear I wear is clean and in good repair. Otherwise, what if I was hit by a car? The hospital emergency room staff would take one look at my torn, dirty underwear and decide that my mother didn't really love me."

Further exploration of this material aligned the menacing storm with the threatened automobile accident. For Sidney, protecting mother from being upset had priority over taking care of himself. In reclaiming the natural power of the storm as his own, he was able to identify many other distasteful projections in the dream as mother-dependent attitudes of his false self. Consciously, he clung to an image of himself as too cultured to be subject to the anger displayed by ordinary people. He imagined that he was a unique creature, so specially sensitive that everyone must admire him. Examination of his dream revealed the underside of this idealized portrait. During the sessions that followed analysis of that dream, he began to pay attention to his hidden image of himself as a uselessly fragile and misshapenly grotesque creature. The projected "hand-painted yellow pansies" symbolized his secret fears that he might turn out to be "a precious, cowardly homosexual."

It took a while before Sidney was able to understand that sexual identity was *not* the central pivot of his self-definition. He was *not* a homosexual, but even if he had been, it need not have implied any lack of genuine worth or courage. Lacking the role model and guidance that a strong, supportive father could have provided, he was uncertain about what it meant to be a full-grown adult male. Even so, he had to find ways to make the transition from the precious position of being his mama's boy to the more ordinary state of becoming his own man. The transformation first required that he grieve his losses. Only then would he be able to identify and reclaim as his own much of what he had previously projected.

174

Continued immersion in the dreamwork reclamation of projections can itself result in the emergence of yet another hidden aspect of personality. After a time, we may become aware of the inner guide who is the dreaming self. As Jung tells us:

Within each one of us there is another whom we do not know. He speaks to us in dreams and tells us how differently *he* sees us from how *we* see ourselves. When we find ourselves in an insolubly difficult situation, this stranger in us can sometimes show us a light which is more suited than anything else to change our attitude fundamentally, namely just that attitude which had led us into the difficult situation.[12]

The focus of my own shifting attention alternates between dedicated devotion to my true self and deceitful collaboration with my false self. During the periods of self-betrayal, I deliberately ignore all coded communications from my own dreaming self. Fearful that they will expose my fraudulence, I refuse to listen to the helpful nightly messages from this secret ally. Whenever I am willing and able to listen to my dreaming self, my daytime life becomes clearer and richer. Sometimes it even becomes easier. Undistorted by reason, logic, and conventional wisdom, my night vision affords a clear perspective as far as the imagination can see.

At first I did not recognize that inner guide as it appeared within my dream encounter with the wolf.[13] My most immediate level of understanding of that dream was as the revelation of projections of some significant aspects of my shadow. At that interpretive level, the darkness of the night pictures how vast and ominous I imagine to be the dark side of myself that is hidden from my waking awareness. The Cape Ann seascape is the hard, cold, cruelly Gothic covert aspect of my personality.

Usually I pictured myself as a decent generous human being. At the time of the dream, I could only understand the wolf as a projection of the evil hidden within me. What a shameless fraud I had been to pretend I was so good when, all the while, the real me was a rapacious beast. Reclaiming the wolf as my own dark brother shattered the surface complacency of my self-serving pretense of civilized virtue. Acknowledging my own predatory ways meant paying attention to aspects of my behavior that I usually either ignore or try to justify. These deceptions allow me to maintain the idealized image of myself as a heroic figure. So long as my pretense goes unchallenged, I can deny my capacity for occasional brutality and/or my more frequent self-serving disregard for anyone's needs but my own.

This unbalanced interpretation of my dream made me feel awful. The destructively predatory nature of my wolf side threatened to discredit all that I consciously valued about myself. I tried to redeem my battered self-esteem by forcing a more acceptable interpretation. My most consistently positive self-image is that of myself as psychotherapist who is a sort of Santa Claus to the bad children.

I could see that my dream held the promise of support for that more comfortable vision of myself. Hoping to renew my shaky self-esteem, I focused on the more promising underside of the archetypal wolf. Even my shadow had a shadow of its own. Though the wolf's primary image is that of a ravaging killer, the destroyer's Double appears in the form of the wolf as nurturing mother. The complementary imagery of myself as having been a feral child[14] allowed me to identify lovingly with the shadow side of the wolf as she who is Mother-of-Outcasts.

Certainly, this maternal aspect of the dream projection was more congruent with my idealized image of myself. The legendary wolf nursed Romulus and Remus so that they might eventually found Rome. As a therapist I have often imagined myself as she whose good mothering rescues banished children and restores their rightful heritage.

Temporarily reassured, I set aside my growing preoccupation with this wolf imagery and refocused my explorations on the continuing stock of dreams that subsequent nights provided. Many weeks had passed before I began to appreciate how much more my wolf dream had to tell me. Without understanding why, again and again I was drawn back to this encounter with my shadow. I became obsessed with trying to decide once and for all if this wolf dream was good news or if it was bad news. Was I to understand it as an indictment of my evil nature or as a confirmation of my decency?

It was not until I surrendered to the realization that my questions were unanswerable that I began to understand that the shifting contradictory interpretations were themselves a commentary on who I am. The wolf of my dreams is mercurial and many-sided. Once unmasked, the changing expressions of its Janus face will not remain fixed.

When within the dream I first encountered this shape-shifting creature, I mistook the wolf for a dog. The following morning, I interpreted my "error" as a warning that the domestication of my own dangerous instinctual nature was tentative and unreliable. Lost and alone in the vast darkness of the barren Cape Ann tundra, I struggled with my need to make friends with this fearful beast. I felt myself forced either to continue living the isolated life of the solitary lone wolf or to risk losing my individual identity by choosing to run with the pack.

The projection of myself as wolf was a compelling composite of the destructive and nurturant, of the wild and the tamed, of the solitary and the communal. I became more and more fascinated with this unyieldingly contradictory image. It was during this hauntingly kaleidoscopic period that someone who cares about me chose to present me with a wolf book.[15] Just when I needed it most, without conscious awareness of how it would serve me, she offered me a wondrous volume of the wolf archetype as it appears in science and in superstition and as it is experienced both through the eyes of the naturalist and of the primitive. No matter how far removed from the wild most of us are, all of our lives remain subtly colored by mythic figures and primordial archetypes. It behooves us to pay attention to these shadowy beasts. In this life, I am no wilderness-wise hunter. Even so, if I remain out of touch with the wolf that wanders through the wilds of my unconscious, I abandon that nocturnal beast at great risk to my civilized, daytime conscious self.

177

Gradually I discovered that the more I was able to accept the undivided continuity between my conscious self and my shadow, the more my dreaming self became available to guide me. Now I understand that it is only when my personality is undivided and my self unsplit that I come into full psychological power. When I am sufficiently self-accepting to decline choosing between one side of myself and another, I can experience myself as a creature *both* of the darkness *and* of the light. Whenever I limit my identity to one or to the other, I risk losing out on opportunities that exist only in the borderland. Between polarities that only *seem* mutually exclusive is a place where I may stand undiminished by projections.

During this period of exploring the borderlands of my consciousness, I had a dream confirming the need to reconcile aspects of myself that had so long seemed irrevocably in opposition. The dream came on the night before I was to spend time with a close friend. He too is a psychotherapist. Both drawn to life in the shadows, we often exchange dreams.

At this time, we were both nearing our watershed fiftieth birthdays. He spoke of a recent series of dreams that he experienced as related to that transition. He remembered clearly having had the dreams, but could not recall just what their content was. The structural form of the dreams had been simply that of performing a number of familiar, routine tasks. The emotional tone was matter of fact. He understood these as "working-through" dreams in which his dreaming self was taking care of business in a way that did not require supervision by his waking self.

My own contribution in this exchange was also that of a dream that retained a clear formal structure though its contents were obscure. All that remained in my daytime recollection was having dreamed of a series of things, events, or people that had appeared one after another, each taking the place of the one before. I remember being surprised at first that female images had alternated with the males. After a while, that seemed natural to me.

178

Throughout the dream, I understood that all of the images bore the same name. It may be that I awoke just as I was about to speak the name. (In retrospect, I now imagine that it would have been unalterably destructive for me to have assigned the name exclusively to any one of the images.)

As I tried to reconstruct the dream so that I could better share it with my friend, my associations were of a machine that rotated its many interchangeable parts. There was something about the many parts that lent to them the shape and configuration of a deck of tarot cards dealt out for a prophetic reading. Now it seems to me that it was more like a self-propelled wheel of fortune. Like my friend's "working-through" dreams, this too had a matter-of-fact quality, a disinterested tone of just this and that, thus and so. It was just the way it was. Nothing more to it.

The process of beginning to experience my many projections as no more than different faces of the same self was a big help. Undivided, I felt better prepared to meet whatever life held in store. For far too long I had been split three ways: high, wide, and frequently. Divided, I had experienced much of my projected personal power as if it were outside of me. Up against these unrecognized aspects of myself, I often felt desperately unprepared, painfully inadequate, and needlessly overwhelmed. Whenever I could, I fooled others by exaggeratedly striking my competent warrior pose. During the day, sometimes I even fooled myself. But at night, again and again, the larger-than-life daylight deceptions yielded to the shadowy revelations of my most recurrent nightmares.

Everyone has bad dreams that interrupt sleep's restorative renewing rest. These awful dreams express disowned thought, feelings, and wishes. The sleeper needs to recognize these disavowals but "the ego hates to admit that it doesn't know everything."[16] Some messages from the unconscious are more disturbing than others. The nightmare may include the partially disguised breakthrough of visions so foreign to our conscious self-image that they pose a catastrophic threat. Still other dreams become nightmares simply because they are incomplete. We have not seen them through to the finish. As in a bad acid trip, it is only the frantic flight itself that terrifies.

Some dreams recur repeatedly. Whether nightmares or less disturbing encounters with the unconscious, they underscore central unresolved motifs in each of our lives. All through my adult years, every couple of months I have the same awful dream. The details vary but the plot structure is consistent. The dreadful quality of the experience never changes.

Typically, the dream begins with my hurrying along a crowded corridor of one or the other of the oppressive institutions in which I have done time. The setting is a composite of elementary school, high schools, and the university in which I studied, the military in which I served, plus the reformatories, prisons, and mental hospitals where I have worked. I am rushing along the corridor under duress, involuntarily carried along by the throng, helplessly headed toward some preordained place, and not at all sure what the hell I'm doing there. Then all at once I find myself herded into the place in which the ordeal is to be held.

The event is always a ceremonial rite of transition that will establish or confirm my identity. Most often this ritual occurs symbolically within the context of a German foreign language course. I took German in college. It was my worst subject. The university required completion of two years of a language. In the case of people like myself who didn't do well, they made an exception. If in the first two years you did poorly enough to demonstrate that you were unsuited to studying that language, then they required that you take a third year! Studying German for three years seemed as though it would take forever.

Along with others who also seem too old to be students, I dream of seating myself at one of those combination desk/chairs that always seem too small for me. Placing the heavy book that I have been carrying on the desk surface, I look expectantly toward the instructor. He seems overbearingly authoritarian. I am shocked to hear him announce that this is the last class meeting of the term. Today we will write our final exams. Hurriedly, he passes out the examination papers and the blue books in which we are to write our answers. It is the last class of the second year of German. If I don't get a good grade I will have to undergo yet another year of study.

My attention is drawn to the massive textbook that sits unopened on my desktop. All at once I am struck by the full impact of my situation. As if for the first time, I realize that during all the many months the course has gone on, I have not yet once cracked this alien tome. In desperation I seize the heavy book from the desktop, open it for the first time, and begin to try to cram frantically through hundreds of pages dense with unfamiliar German words. If only the instructor distributes the examination papers slowly enough, perhaps miraculously somehow I will have time to prepare myself adequately for taking the test. At about that point I always waken feeling shamefully insufficient as a human being.

The working-through of my wheel-of-fortune dream unified the opposing aspects revealed in my wolf dream. Some weeks later, my German examination dream recurred and for the first time it came to a happy conclusion. It began and progressed in the familiarly excruciating manner, but this time it ended with the overbearing, authoritarian instructor transformed into a gently androgynous guru. (S)he approached me, warm, smiling, and eager to help. All at once I realized that I was no longer just the needy student. This time I was the helpful instructor as well.

When (s)he spoke it was my own voice saying, "I am here to help you prepare. From now on, I will be available whenever you need me. If you no longer demand that I only appear when it's time to test you, then you can count on my being here to teach you." I awoke understanding that I need never again feel so helplessly alone. My newly complete self was both prepared for and sufficient to whatever lay ahead.

NOTES, CHAPTER 12

1. Charles Horton Cooley, *Human Nature and the Social Order*, rev. ed. (New York: Charles Scribner's Sons, 1922), pp. 183–185.
2. Some aspects of the self stand in opposition apart from being judged. I

experience neither as good nor bad so much as simply contradicting one another. In that case, I may further divide my personality in the interest of
maintaining a reassuringly consistent self-concept.

3. D. W. Winnicott, *The Maturational Processes and the Facilitating Environment: Studies in Theory of Emotional Development* (New York: International Universities Press, 1965), p. 186.

4. Tennessee Williams, "Desire and the Black Masseur," in *One Arm and
Other Stories* (New York: New Directions, 1967), pp. 83–94.

5. Ibid., p. 83.

6. Ibid., p. 87.

7. Ibid., p. 90.

8. Ibid.

9. Ibid., p. 93.

10. Jack Downing and Robert Mamorstein, eds., *Dreams and Nightmares:
A Book of Gestalt Therapy Sessions* (New York: Harper & Row, Perennial
Library, 1973).

11. Yiddish word for treasured decorative pieces usually displayed on
shelves or in a "chotchka cabinet."

12. C. G. Jung, *Prakstische Seelenheilkunde Zentralblatt für Psychother-
apie*, IX 1936), 3:184–187 (review of G. R. Heyer), in Yolande Jacobi, ed.,
Psychological Reflections: An Anthology of the Writings of C. G. Jung
(New York: Harper & Row, 1961), p. 67.

13. See pp. 26–27.

14. Feral children are those wild boys and girls believed to have been raised
by nurturing female wolves after their human parents abandoned them.

15. Barry Holstum Lopez, *Of Wolves and Men* (New York: Charles
Scribner's Sons, 1978).

16. Donald Lathrop, "The Dream World," *Voices*, vol. 14, no. 1, Spring
1978, p. 11.

CHAPTER 13

Return to the Borderland

Increased self-acceptance always makes us feel better. We can feel the tensions ease even when this acceptance takes the seemingly superficial form of musing on the frailties of human nature. Calling up the reassurances of such age-old adages as "Nobody's perfect," "Everyone makes mistakes," and "Tomorrow's another day," we forgive ourselves our imperfections, make allowances for our errors, and grant ourselves another chance. Forgoing perfectionistic ideals, we increase our self-acceptance and restore our self-esteem. By reducing the demands of what we *should be*, we can live more comfortably with what we *are*. Paradoxically, it is this acceptance of what is that increases our chances of *becoming* all that we might yet be. Simply scaling our image down to life size eases tensions, spares us perfectionist self-recriminations, and adds to the satisfactions afforded by ordinary everyday accomplishments.

The reclaiming of projections is a more complex form of self-acceptance. In addition to the rewards of simple relinquishment of perfectionist ideals, it offers the freedom of the imagination, the release of creative power, and the enrichment of everyday experience. Restoring to consciousness these previously repressed parts of the self releases psychological resources previously relegated to the unconscious.

Completion of this form of self-acceptance takes a little longer than a single lifetime. It is an uneven process. We cannot will its stops and starts. Getting on with it requires that we give up the illusion that our waking rational consciousness is in control. The more we surrender to the topsy-turvy spirit of the borderland shadow life, the greater the subjective rewards. We need only learn to tolerate the reconciliation of opposites, the experience of multiple realities, and the understanding that all that we have banished as not-self must also be accepted as true self.

It is by no means as simple as deciding that I am *really* exactly the opposite of what I have always imagined myself to be. That reversal is no more than a psychoanalytic fallacy: the mistaken beliefs that only what is hidden is real, and that only what has been repressed is true. Instead, as in my wolf dream, I must accept that all of the seemingly contradictory parts of myself are worth something. I must learn to value every bit of who I am.

I dare not ignore my shadow self. At the same time, I cannot afford to discard my conscious everyday vision of who I am. Worse yet, full acceptance of both requires my honoring the paradox that what is weakness in one may be strength in the other. Whatever seems most foolish to my everyday consciousness will serve as my wisest counsel when I am seeing from the inside out.

The shadow wolf in my dream increases in value for me only as I give up insisting that it be simply one thing or another. My dream wolf is truly a werewolf, human by day *and* beast by night. It is foolish to ask, "What is it . . . really?" Like the self, the wolf is a classically contradictory creature. Both are vibrantly mercurial, ever-shifting shapes that defy definition by any single list of congruent traits.

Hunting cultures admire and honor the wolf for its courage, its predatory skills, and its endurance. Agricultural societies despise the very same wolf for its cowardice, its stupidity, and its brutality. Some groups see the beast as destructively rapacious and dangerously cunning, while in the folklore of others it appears as a frivolous, gullible prankster. Viewed alternately as the ravenous killer of innocents and as the nurturant mother of outcasts, the wolf can be defined simultaneously both as a cynically ascetic loner and as a devotedly loyal member of the pack.

The wolf is truly a twilight figure, ultimately resistant to being reduced to simply one thing or another. In my dream, at first I mistook the beast for its tamer counterpart, the dog. My conscious self would have liked nothing better than to have transformed this wild creature of the night into a familiar daytime companion. It was as though I believed that to domesticate my shadow into "man's best friend," all I needed to do was housebreak the beast. But even within the dream experience I became aware of my daylight counterphobic response to dogs. Paradoxically, this very denial attests to my fearful secret recognition of the wolf shadow that trails Fido to its master's hearthside.

The archetypal wolf cannot be reduced to this or that, and no more. Both the wolf and the self at times appear as archetypes.[1] As such, neither can ever be comfortably homogenized. Self-acceptance eases tensions, affords psychological power, and provides a greater feeling of completeness. But reaping these rewards requires learning to accept a self that remains ambiguous no matter how closely it is scrutinized. Fluid, active, filled with unresolvable contradictions, it is the nature of the self to remain beyond the ego's willful demand for a logically consistent system.

This radical expansion of self-acceptance requires the voluntary suspension of disbelief. Both the rule of reason and the security of a single reality must yield to immersion in imagination. But first the familiar everyday ego must be set aside, the most difficult step of all.

Personality is the modern counterpart of the soul. As a latterday form of spiritual growth, psychological self-acceptance requires risk and sacrifice. The same painfully elusive simple truth must be learned yet another time: you cannot hope to find your self unless you first are willing to lose your self.

For as long as you can remember, your self-image has been highly selective both in what it includes and in what it clearly excludes. Now you must risk thinking the unthinkable. All that you have always rejected as not-you, you must now accept as valued parts of your expanded vision of who you are.

It is as if you are being asked to relive willingly some of the experiences of the first three years of your life. This calls for a return to the borderland. You must be willing to return to the mercurial experience of life before the boundaries of the self had yet been definitely established. It is a timeless time when there was as yet no clear and final separation between past and present, nor between dream and reality. Distinctions between what is you and what is the other are indefinite and ever shifting.

We each encounter many opportunities for this sort of personal growth. Any experience that alters our everyday state of consciousness, unsettles our ordinary sense of reality, or challenges our unexamined identity, opens a doorway to the rest of the self. Ingestion of mind-altering drugs, depth psychotherapy, fasting, and meditation are all voluntary pursuits of these ego-transcendent experiences.

Other, more painful access is sometimes thrust upon us in the form of stress situations. These, too, can serve our desire for personal growth. One such growth opportunity offered to me by situational stress was the unforgettable ordeal of infantry basic training. In fairly short order, I was reduced from the status of a confident young member of the power elite helping professions to that of an inept green recruit who would be lucky to make it through basic training. Unwillingly, I relinquished more and more of the valued image of who I was. As my self-esteem dwindled my panic grew. I realized that many of the other young draftees were having at least as hard a time as I. Knowing that helped, but not a lot.

A chronic misfit named Harold stood out as the most confused trainee of the platoon. At first, this awkward, bewildered

186

character seemed simply stupid. His situation turned out to be more poignant than that. Harold was bright enough, but he felt completely lost outside of the protective shelter in which he had lived as a civilian.

Before being drafted, this schizoid character had led a marginal life. He was able to manage by clinging to his mother as if he were a perennially helpless dependent child. At the age of twenty-three, his life of peaceful isolation was largely free of friends or outside demands. For many years he had worked in the sheltering atmosphere of a small-town soda-bottling factory run by his uncle. All he had to do was to carry cases of soda from one part of the factory to another. Wistfully, he said of his job: "It was really swell. There was nothing to interrupt my daydreams."

In the basic training unit, he soon became the primary scapegoat of the training cadre. He could not do close-order drill without bumping into the other men, nor handle a rifle without dropping it in the dirt. Again and again the corporal in charge would single out Harold for public ridicule. As if parade-ground and firing-range shaming was not enough, Harold was under a continual barrage of criticism in the barracks as well. He was hounded mercilessly for not shining his boots, for not making his bed properly, for being out of uniform, and just generally for being out to lunch.

Not understanding who it was they were asking him to become, Harold grew increasingly frightened and depressed. I was afraid that he would go crazy and end up in a psychiatric ward for the rest of his life. In part, I was trying to reassert my own status as a helping professional. Partly, I identified with Harold because I feared that if I lost my self, I too would lose my mind.

Then one day I saw the creative possibility of voluntarily surrendering my self. I approached Harold and shyly asked if he would help me with my difficulties. Candidly, I told him that in the midst of the constant harassment of basic training I was having trouble remembering who I was. I asked if he would be willing to help protect me from the disorienting criticism and abuse of the training officers.

Fearing that I was asking more than he could manage, Harold was understandably suspicious. I assured him that all I wanted was that he check each morning to make sure that I had shined my boots and properly made my bed. His initial distrust soon gave way to a confident glow of pleasure. He told me that this was a job he was certain that he could handle, and that I could count on him to make sure that I did what the army expected of me.

Just as he promised, each morning for the remaining weeks in basic training Harold watched over me. He was a wonderful caretaker, and I was a trustingly dependent ward. We each enjoyed our new roles. Our willingness to reclaim seemingly alien aspects of ourselves was enormously helpful in getting us through this identity-threatening stress situation. Since then, occasionally allowing myself to become Harold has continued to serve me well. I can only hope that Harold's accepting me as his Double has served him as well.

External stress situations often offer opportunties for making lasting changes in the boundaries of self-acceptance. However, the opportunity-providing pressure need not come from the outside. Our sense of who we are can be as readily challenged by internal processes as by situational distress. Subjective crises marked by anxiety, by doubt, and by despair often signal periods of personal unrest sufficiently unsettling to allow the opportunity for personal growth. It is during such periods of internal disruption that some people seek psychotherapy. Whether the familiar image of the self is called into question by external circumstances or by internal distress, a time of confused identity can be useful. Without temporary disorientation about who we are, it is not possible to effect lasting changes in the limits of our self-acceptance. Ritual preparations for spiritual growth always include unsettlingly disorienting experiences. If the set and the setting are conducive, fasting, isolation, chanting, and meditation all can evoke visions and revelations that are experienced as an identity-changing death and rebirth of the soul. In order to continue growing we must learn that "personality, no matter how habitual, is a constantly renewed choice."[2]

It is the same for all of us. Whether out of abundance we submit voluntarily to a program of expanded self-awareness, or in time of crisis we go kicking and screaming that we cannot stand life as it is, personal growth requires that again and again we must renew our work on the self. And the deepest, most lasting of this work always requires a return to the borderland.

What sort of territory is this borderland? Like any transitional zone between contrasting areas of experience, this psychological borderland has the threshold aura of power and mystery, as well as the Janus propensity for both good and evil. The obscured boundaries promote a period of disorder, traditionally intensified by otherwise prohibited mischief. From the ancient orgies that heralded winter's end and spring's beginning to residual contemporary rituals marking seasonal transitions, boundaries are crossed in an atmosphere of ambiguity and abandon.

On Halloween, negative and positive prospects stand side by side as "trick or treat." Unbounded disorder is reflected in the obliteration of daylight distinctions between fantasy and reality. Dressing up in each others' clothes, boys and girls eliminate the "normal" separation of the sexes. Even the boundary between the living and the dead is irreverently mocked when these little costumed creatures of night appear at neighbors' doors masquerading as ghosts and goblins.

Structurally paralleling social and seasonal thresholds, the psychological borderland too is a shadowy underworld, a lawless frontier beyond the conventional authority of reason, manners, and morality. In the borderland, nothing is unthinkable. Everything is permitted. Amid this antic anarchy, facts are replaced by metaphors. Right and wrong are ignored in favor of shameless opportunism. It is a topsy-turvy, left-handed world that includes all that is ordinarily excluded from consciousness. Without our access to the borderland, these unaccepted aspects instead

189

operate in unconscious ways, chronically undermining the "sensible" intentions of the daytime self.

Though this destructive division of the personality is greatest in those seriously deprived of good-enough mothering during the years prior to developing a cohesive self-image, no child grows up entirely free of emotional damage. Few end up vertically split into pathologically divided personalities, but in order to survive every one of us has had to relinquish some aspects of who we are. Restorative self-acceptance requires *voluntary* return to a borderland that structurally parallels the archaic experience of those early years when the self first was forming. Ironically, the damaging effects of shaming suffered at that time can be healed now only by the shameless reclaiming of all that we earlier disowned.

Here in the borderland we must once again reclaim all that our daytime consciousness usually considers bad, awkward, embarrassing, or in some other way unacceptable. Not only must we accept the *dark* shadow as part of us, but the bright one as well. The hidden grandiose self too must be revealed in all its glory. We must learn to welcome *all* of the figures in our dreams. No one of these projections is either too bad or too good to belong to us. If we want a more complete self, we must make every one of these strangers feel at home in our personalities.

It is never possible for the complete self to be conscious at one time. We cannot focus clearly on any particular aspect without the rest more obscurely receding into the shadowy background. In the borderland, we see most clearly by squinting in the "divine primordial half-light"[3] of our dreaming consciousness. It is only in this psychological twilight that our otherwise antagonistic polarities can be seen existing side by side as opposites in the absence of conflict.

The borderland is the marginal area of the magician. All the fun emerges from allowing the illusion. It is the demimonde of the clown, of the freak, and of the carnival hustler. Here we find juggling, sleight of hand, and games of chance. In the waking life nothing is quite what it seems. Paradoxically, in

190

the borderland, what you see is what you get! Along this mid-way, I may discover that I am something of a trickster myself. If so, I must resist any temptation to try to reform. Instead, at least till dawn, I must allow myself to be transformed into the Prince of Thieves.

If I am to feel more at home in the borderland, I must not restrict myself to tourist visits in season. Instead, whenever an opportunity presents itself, I must veer to the left, choosing the odd and the unusual over everything my waking consciousness finds more natural and familiar. My daytime weaknesses are my nighttime strengths. If my wounds are to heal, it is not my bandages, but my open running sores that must be exposed. From the perspective of the shadows, the self-righteous daylight ego's losses are the underworld self's gains.

The more of my life I live in the light of daytime consciousness, the more I share that life with the shadowy Double of my secret second self. Like you, I already live a life of duplicity, cheating, and weaseling out of the responsibility of owning all of myself. By acknowledging the deceptive ways of my already double life, I can allow myself access to the space between my visible and my hidden self.

Slipping into this twilight zone, I enter the borderland. Here I am in a position to barter for reclamation of the rest of myself. To get back all that I have lost, I need only assume the unheroic attitude of shameless opportunist. In this marginal turf of the street-wise hustler, it is not might or right that allows me to make out. It all depends on my wily ways of changing my shape.

The narrower, more rigidly restricted my sense of who I am, the more likely that rather than score myself, I will once more play the innocent mark, the self-righteous victim. Life in the borderland is a restless, rootless hustler's existence. Like living as a werewolf, it calls for continuous change not only in shape, but in place as well. Always on the road between here and there, this twilight trek involves living a life half sane, half mad, but always marvelous and mysterious.

191

It is a way peculiar to the night, only appearing by day as "a sudden darkening or an enigmatic smile."[4] It is the way of paradox, of new awareness that, at the same time, things can both be and not be, of polarities at peace, of opposites not in need of reconciliation. Like the Way of the Tao, it is not graspable except when I weaken my hold. This midway and marketplace of the soul is a place to barter and to bargain. It is not a place I can visit without risking being tricked, cheated, or led astray.

Once there, as an exercise in shameless opportunism, I must be ready to run my own scam. This is no place for the proper, the complacent, or the self-righteous. If I am to make out in the borderland, I must be willing to act undignified, to appear vulgar, even to risk being repulsive. As a borderland hustler, I may occasionally have to work to get what I am after, but more often I will depend on guile and on luck.

The borderland is not a safe place for the prudish or the squeamish, the orderly or the sensible, or for any others who represent the repressive side of the self. It is a scene of scandal, an area of excess, of abandon, and of decadence, in which no personal quality is too undignified, too vulgar, or too disgusting to be acknowledged as my own.

No matter how awful, I must reclaim every disowned projection as belonging to me. Radically expanded self-acceptance depends on this subjectively shameless borderland attitude. This archaic attitude does not yet distinguish between what I am and what I should be. It is no more than the freeing of my imagination. That I choose to peer into my own shadows need not concern anyone else. Recognition of my own dark brother as part of me does not demand that others also must accept the wolf that I am.

But if I become shamelessly accepting of so much within myself that is conventionally considered immoral, what are the implications of all this for how I am to treat other people? First of all, though every unthinkable aspect of myself must be identified, not all of them need be indulged. The only constraint required by this sort of self-acceptance is the negative ethic that

192

I *not* do unto others anything that I would *not* want done to myself.

The narcissistic ethic of the "Me Generation"[5] has been deservedly criticized as shallow, indulgent, sensation-seeking expression of whatever feels good at the moment with flagrant disregard for how this might make other people feel. Paradoxically, while the self-acceptance that comes of my return to the borderland puts me in touch with my own hedonistic grandiosity, it also demands my recognition of how insignificant I am to almost everyone else in the world. When I lose sight of how much less important I am to anyone other than myself, I am tempted to demand that they attend adoringly to everything and anything I say or do. Like a toddler, I expect everyone else to be as excited about the wonderfulness of my bowel movements as Mommy and I are.

The self-acceptance that comes of the return to the borderland leaves me more respectful of other people. Reclamation of my negative projections allows me to experience others less judgmentally. In the absence of the disowned personal characteristics that I usually attribute to them, I can more easily recognize that all of the other people have equivalent selves of their own. I use others as containers for the unacceptable parts of my self in order to deny how disappointing, inconsistent, imperfect, at times inadequate my own personality sometimes seems to me. Feeling proud of or ashamed of another person means that his or her separation from my self is incomplete. The residual merger is less love than it is emotional exploitation.[6]

Nonexploitive relationships between adults depend on well-defined boundaries between one self and another. When it is clear that I am I and that you are you, I have no need to manipulate your image of me. Retaining the power of my own autonomous self-image, I understand that my feeling good depends not on your reaction to me, but on how I live my life. So it is that the more clearly I remain in charge of myself, the more you can trust that whatever I offer you is freely given. My ability to give will be proportionate to my freedom to withhold from you. If I try to please you to complete myself, it will cost you something. If I do so only when it pleases me, you get to keep whatever I give you.

The most trustworthy place for others in my life is that which I set aside out of an abundance of private space for myself. The Hasidic parable of the window and the curtain is instructive.[7] As a houseguest of his respected rabbi, a young student was troubled when he noticed that the curtains had been drawn across his window. When his host asked the cause of his troubled glance, the student replied, "If you want people to look in, then why the curtains? And if you do not want them to look in, then why the window?"

"When I want someone I love to look in," answered the rabbi, "then I draw aside the curtain."

Any attempt to resolve my difficulties with others must begin with my recognizing the ways in which I may be using them as containers for my projections. I must expand my idealized image of who I am to include all I might wish I was not. Only then can I be confident that I will treat other people with the respect due their wholly separate souls. Otherwise I am sure to hold them in the contempt accorded devices for completing my own divided self.

Contaminated by political pressures, misled by conventional wisdom, and distorted by my idealized image of who I would like to believe I am, my waking consciousness alone is not much help in gaining the needed expansion of the frontiers of my self-acceptance. On my return trips to the borderland, my dreaming self is a far more reliable inner guide. As a way of immersing me in the reclamation of my projections, the writing of this book is also part of that work on my own expanded self-acceptance. But while playing the author affords opportunities for personal growth, it is up to the shameless opportunist in me to grasp these options.

One night early in the writing of this book, I had a sequence of borderland dreams. Still focused on external guides and too reliant on rational solutions to personal problems, I almost missed seizing the opportunities these dreams provided. At about 3:00 A.M., I awoke from my first remembered dream of this night. It took place in the mountains at a beautiful resort. Though in my waking life I do not play tennis, I had just won a tennis tournament. I don't remember the tournament itself, but I do recall both the celebrative atmosphere as I was awarded the trophy and my great pleasure in receiving it. There was more to the dream, but the rest is no longer available to me.

On awakening I felt energized and ready to set out to do something important. The now forgotten details of the dream made me aware that some of the insights I needed for the writing of this new book were contained in the pages of a manuscript that a friend had sent me earlier. I knew that I would not be able to fall asleep again without checking his manuscript. To make sure I would not forget the dream's instructions, I arose in the night and went to my files to retrieve the pertinent pages of the manuscript. There and then, I sat down at my desk and read through those pages. Much to my embarrassment, it turned out that they contained nothing that was at all relevant or useful to my conception of my own book!

I felt disappointed and bewildered. At that point I could not yet consciously understand that the dream message had to do with giving up seeking instruction from sources outside of myself. In my confusion, wisely I stumbled back to bed. Later that night, I had a second dream. Although it too took place in the mountains, it was clearly a second dream rather than a continuation of the first. There had been some natural disaster, caused, it seemed, by torrential rains. Everywhere I turned there were great mudslides. Trying to get from one place to another was both difficult and dangerous.

There was some place I had to go. I felt stuck. Then ahead of me I saw a small walking bridge at which a few people had lined up hoping to safely cross the border. At the access to the bridge stood a gatekeeper. He kept the people in their proper places in line, admitting them one by one so that they might cross

195

the bridge. I felt delighted to have found a way to get where I wanted to go.

I took my place in line but when my turn came the gatekeeper stopped me. He said, "You can't use this bridge. You don't really belong here. You're just a tourist. This bridge is only for the locals."

I felt a surge of personal power rising up in me as I made my claim on him. "But it is you who don't understand," I insisted. "You must recognize me for who I am. I'm the guy who won the tennis tournament in the *first* dream!"

In a friendly, apologetic way, the gatekeeper conceded, saying, "Oh, I'm sorry. At first I didn't see that it was you. Of course *you* can use the bridge any time." I crossed the bridge, awakened, and felt fine all day.

My sense of personal power was repeatedly renewed as I gradually came to better understand the dreams. The mountain-top is my place of enlightenment. Life in the communal valley offers the support of social contact and of conventional wisdom, but only in ascending to the peaks can the self be alone with the self. In the solitude of release from attachment to the expectations of others, the self enters the borderland in which any one person is a majority.

Winning the tennis tournament reveals how little of my complete Self is realized by my waking consciousness. The celebrative atmosphere heralds the breakthrough, a transition into the borderland, my triumph over the limitations of the possible, the practical, and the rational. It announces my transformation into the shape shifter.

The natural catastrophes are life's uncontrollable disruptions. The mudslides that are so hard to get around symbolize my responsive depressions. Though I always experience the depressions as painful and limiting, I understand that they sometimes serve as the only way of sufficiently disrupting my waking complacency to allow further personal growth. The bridge of access to the borderland is appropriately guarded by the gatekeeper aspect of the archetypal self. He will not admit tourists who

196

come in search of souvenirs and entertainment. Only committed regulars are welcome. The credentials of entry are a willingness to stay long enough to learn the customs, to speak the language like a native, and to make the borderland your home.

The aspect of myself that feels most at home there claimed its place by displaying the regional custom of shameless opportunism. Triumphing over the constraints of my everyday consciousness, I protested, "Hey everybody, I'm a winner!" Undivided, I stepped across from one dream to another demanding recognition by the gatekeeper, access to the borderland, and acceptance as "a local."

There are predictable phases in the life cycle during which development of the self is naturally expanded and consolidated. The two most obvious growth phases take place in toddlers and then again in adolescents. Acknowledging these primary developmental sequences need not obscure recurrent possibilities for further differentiation of the self throughout an entire lifetime.

At those times when my life is most disrupted, I again have the opportunity to expand the limits of my acceptance sufficiently to allow further development of my self. It is at just those times when "things fall apart; [and] the centre cannot hold"[8] that it is myself I must remake. To the extent that I can tolerate its changing shape, my self is renewable. Only if I am willing to risk losing my everyday waking self can I find that more imaginatively resourceful aspect that is my borderland self.

After repeated journeys into the borderland, the self becomes partly autonomous in its transformations. Then like legendary shape changers, shamans, and medieval magicians, my waking ego can depend on the unsupervised shadow self inducing whatever trances and evolving whatever illusions I may need to further the expansion of my consciousness.

The only creative act necessary to the continuing development of my self is willingness to peer more deeply into the shadows so I may see more clearly. But these transformations cannot be gained without cost. They require my learning to live the rest of my days in the ambiguity of knowing that *of all that I am, I am also the opposite.* I cannot rid myself of my demons without risking that my angels will flee along with them.

NOTES, CHAPTER 13

1. C. G. Jung, *The Archetypes and the Collective Unconscious,* in *The Collected Works of C. G. Jung,* vol. 9, Part 1, 2nd ed. (Princeton, N. J.: Princeton University Press, Bollingen Series XX, 1968).

2. William Butler Yeats, *A Vision* (New York: Macmillan Publishing Co., 1938), p. 84. A reissue with the author's final revisions.

3. James Hillman, "Senex and Puer: An Aspect of the Historical and Psychological Present," in James Hillman, Henry A. Murray, Tom Moore, James Baird, Thomas Cowan, and Randolph Severson, *Puer Papers* (Dallas, Tex.: Spring Publications, 1979), p. 13.

4. Rafael Lopez-Pedraza, *Hermes and His Children* (Zurich, Switzerland: Spring Publications, 1977), p. 9.

5. Christopher Lasch, *The Culture of Narcissism: American Life in an Age of Diminishing Expectations* (New York: W. W. Norton & Co., 1979).

6. The phase of appropriate merger between parent and small child would serve as an exception.

7. Martin Buber, *Tales of the Hasidim: Later Masters* (New York: Schocken Books, 1966), p. 177.

8. William Butler Yeats, "The Second Coming," in *Selected Poems and Two Plays of William Butler Yeats* (updated ed.), ed. and with an introduction by M. L. Rosenthal (New York: Collier Books, 1962), p. 91.